BILLPAYERS' RIGHTS

Fourth Edition

By Attorneys

Ralph Warner, J.D.
Member, California State Bar

Peter Jan Honigsberg, J.D.
Member, New York State Bar

Editorial Assistance: Katherine M. Galvin

950 Parker Street, Berkeley, CA 94710

Nolo Press is committed to keeping its books up-to-date. Each new printing, whether or not it is called a new edition, has been completely revised to reflect latest law changes. This book was printed and updated on the last date indicated below. If this book is out-of-date, do not rely on the information without checking it in a newer edition.

First Edition   April 1974
Second Edition   January 1975
Third Printing   July 1977
Third Edition   June 1979
Fourth Edition   July 1981

Please Read This: We have done our best to give you useful and accurate information concerning debt problems. But please be aware that laws and procedures are constantly changing and are subject to differing interpretations. You have the responsibility to check all material you read here before relying on it. Of necessity, neither Nolo Press nor the authors make any guarantees concerning the information in this book or the use to which it is put.

ISBN 0-917316-34-7

THANK YOU

The kindness and love of many friends sustained us and, in a very real sense, made this book possible. We are particularly grateful for the advice and positive suggestions made by a number of fine lawyers and friends, including Phyllis Eliasberg, Carmen Massey, Scott Noble, Bud Smith and Paul Rosenthal. Paul was originally to have been a co-author of this book but found that his fine new restaurant, The Crossroads, in San Anselmo, took all available energy.

We are also grateful for the friendly advice of Marshal Charles Iverson of Richmond and for the generous help and many excellent suggestions of Ron Chase, the manager of the Co-op Credit Union in Berkeley.

Thanks too to Papa Nolo, Ed Sherman, many of whose graceful words appear in chapter 3, to Malcolm Roberts, everybody's favorite tax guru, and to our good buddy Lynn Smith who had the thankless task of reducing our original chicken scratches to a typed manuscript.

Illustrations:

The engravings first appeared in
Saint Nicholas Magazine (1877, 1878, 1879),
published in New York by Scribner & Co.

Line drawings by
Linda Allison

CONTENTS

INTRODUCTION

Here is a book about the problems that come with owing money and being unable or unwilling to pay it. We tell you exactly what and who you are up against and how you can best deal with your situation. The information given here is known by every credit bureau, bill collector, loan shark, and collection attorney in the country. They use this information consciously and often cynically to squeeze every possible cent out of you. Here, we give you the knowledge to avoid the squeeze where possible, and in many cases to exert a little pressure of your own.

At a time when consumption has become a god and we are taught from birth that large quantities of shiny gadgets will make us happy, most people are in debt. Indeed much of our society seems to be built around the buying and selling of more and more expensive nonsense and might well have a nervous breakdown if people showed signs of not buying things on credit. For most of us it doesn't take much in the way of illness, accident, loss of work, or domestic trouble, etc., to tip the scales so that our burden of debt becomes impossible to carry. When this happens and the notices, phone calls, threats, wage attachments, repossessions, and all the rest begin, we learn quickly how society treats those who fall even a little behind in their ability to pay for their possessions. It isn't very nice. Simply stated, it's brutal, ruthless, and usually effective.

California law has always been favorable to creditors. In the past several years, however, the legislature and courts - at the urgings of consumer and legal aid organizations - have provided greater protection for the person in debt. Here we give you all of that information so that you can use it to protect yourself and plan sensibly for the future.

In writing this book we have had some trouble figuring out the best way to organize all the material. This is partly because different types of debts are treated differently under the law. But it is also partly because people approach life from so many different directions. One person is mostly worried about whether she can wipe out a student loan in bankruptcy, while someone else only cares about the repossession of a pickup truck. All necessary information has been included, but perhaps not in the order you might have chosen. Please pay close attention to the table of contents. You will find it to be a good outline of the whole subject as well as a direction finder for any individual problem. There is nothing hard about the rules and regulations that we discuss, but some overlap a bit and others are a little sticky and technical. You need to relax and get the complete picture before you make any decisions. So read the whole book through and then reread the parts that are of special interest to you.

Some people will feel that this book is overly biased in favor of debtors and that the existence of unscrupulous debtors and honest creditors is overlooked. To this charge we plead guilty. In these pages the creditor appears rather regularly as an ogre. We do not mean that "badness" is necessarily in the nature of creditors. But, since we are writing about problems as seen from the debtor's point of view, we do focus upon all the foul deeds that creditors have been known to do, including misleading advertising, exorbitant interest rates, shoddy goods, and brutal collection practices. Yes, this book is purposely oriented around debtor's problems. Creditors have associations, lobbyists, lawyers and legislators to protect their interests, while debtors have almost no resources. This book is designed to change this imbalance. In short—this is a battle book.

CHAPTER 1

GENERAL THINGS TO KNOW

A. IT'S NOT AS BAD AS YOU THINK

Many people believe that once they get into debt all sorts of terrible things will happen to them. In fact very few of these imagined horrors exist. Being in debt may be unpleasant, but it is not a catastrophe. To start with, you can't be sent to jail for not paying your debts whether you have the money to do so or not*. Debtors' prison no longer exists. In addition most of your property including the equity in your house (if homesteaded) or mobile home, your clothing, your furniture, up to $1,000 in a savings and loan association, $1400 in a credit union, and an inexpensive used car are exempt under California law and can't be taken from you to pay other debts.** (There are a lot more exemptions in addition to the few mentioned here; see chapters 10, 11 and 12 for a complete discussion.)

---

*You can be sent to jail under criminal laws for not paying spousal support (alimony) or child support if, and only if, you have the ability to support and refuse to do so. See chapter 17.

**Of course, no exemption law protects you from losing an item where you have failed to make payments on the item itself, and the item has been put up for security. See chapter 5.

Many types of income are also exempt from attachment, including unemployment, disability, workmen's compensation, social security and welfare benefits. Wages can be attached, but only up to 25% of your pay check and, if you can show that you and/or your family need your pay to live decently, you may be able to get even this portion returned to you (see chapter 10).*

There is no need to put up with harassment by bill collectors. There are now strict rules as to what collectors can and can't do. We will teach you all you need to know about enforcing these rules in chapter 7.

You may decide after reading what follows that your burden of debt is too heavy to ever pay off. If so, you can file bankruptcy and wipe out your bills entirely, or you can arrange to pay them over a long period of time (see chapter 18).

B. ANXIETY

Most of us are raised to believe that a person should pay his debts and that it is somehow immoral not to. We are told that successful, together people have lots of money and possessions, and that people who have neither are failures. This view of life is reinforced often by a society which commonly hands out places in the pecking order solely on the basis of how much money a person has. OK so what else is new—you know all that. But know too that bill collectors are carefully trained to exploit your guilt feelings and are consciously trying to make you feel as miserable as possible. They figure that if they make you feel anxious enough you will scramble to get the money you owe them somehow. If you have a heart attack or develop an ulcer in the meantime—well that's your problem.

When bills pile up and there is no money to pay them, most people get anxious. Their minds return time and time again to the problem of their debts and the fact that they can't be paid. Of course this is a waste of time, but then worrying usually is. Even people who understand intellectually that being a good human being and a rich one are not the same thing, that wealth

---

* Wages can be attached to satisfy child and spousal support debts (Chapter 17). There are also special rules for taxes (Chapter 16).

is as likely to interfere with humanity as to enhance it, get trapped by anxiety. They do this even though they realize that they are hurting themselves far more than the bill collector can.

Getting on top of anxiety and stopping the fretting away of one's life over money worries is a hard, but necessary job. We will help you with some of it by explaining simply what you are and are not up against, and giving you some ideas as to what you can do to help yourself. We can't do the whole job for you, however. Only you can understand that being a loving, wise, giving human being has nothing to do with how much money you owe. Only you can clear yourself of the programming of a million Madison Avenue advertisements and realize that owing a few bills is not the end of the world. Cheer up—wallowing in guilt is a waste of life's beautiful energy.

C. WHAT ABOUT MY CREDIT

If a wise man were required to give away his possessions in their order of importance, so that he shed the least important first, he would certainly get rid of his good credit rating at the start. After all, what is a good credit rating other than a license to buy lots of things you could do without, at prices that exceed their true worth to you, while paying unreasonable amounts of interest for the privilege. Clearly, it makes much better sense to buy less in the first place, and always to buy only those things that you can easily and conveniently afford.

What we mean to say is this. We will discuss the effect different courses of action have on your credit as we go along. But please, please remember that your credit privileges are not worth much to start with and are certainly not worth losing sleep over. It's true that it's difficult to do a few things such as rent a car in a strange city without a credit card, but generally cash will take you where you want to go.* Maybe you won't get there as fast as you would with a little plastic card, but at least when you do arrive it will be your trip.

---

* We favor legislation requiring businesses to accept cash for all transactions and to charge cash customers lower prices.

D. LEGAL JARGON DEFINITIONS

As you read further you will come upon a few terms that you may not be familiar with, or which may have technical legal meanings different from the common ones. Our aim is to simplify, to speak plainly to those without legal training, but it is necessary to use some legal jargon. We will define the meanings of most unfamiliar terms as we go along, but there are a few that we should deal with right now.

Acceleration Clause—Allows the remaining balance due on a contract to be immediately due. Usually this occurs when you miss a payment.

Amortization—Repaying a loan or other debt in installments.

Balloon Payment—The Final payment of an installment contract which is larger than the others. Beware of this one.

Collateral—Additional security given to get a loan. For example, if you buy a dishwasher a finance company may have you list all your furniture on the finance agreement as extra security. If you don't make the payments the finance company will threaten to take (repossess) all your furniture as well as the dishwasher.

Creditor—As used by us, this means a person to whom money is owed. A creditor may be the person who actually lent the money, or he may be someone like the bill collector who is collecting the money for the original creditor.

Debtor—A person who owes money.

Down Payment (deposits)—Money you put down to bind a deal. They are generally not refundable if you back out unless you have a good reason, but generally are refundable if the other party fails to perform.

Co-Signer—The best one word definition that we know for most co-signers is "IDIOT." A co-signer is a person who by signing his name fully obligates himself to pay another person's debt if that person fails to do so, whatever the reason.* The co-signer gets none of the benefits from the transaction (usually some sort of loan) and often, all of the burdens. Should the primary debtor default, the co-signer can be sued if he doesn't pay the debt voluntarily, and is subject to having his wages attached if he doesn't pay the judgment. A person should co-sign only if he is fully prepared to pay the debt if the debtor defaults.

Equity—The dollar amount of your home or other property that you own. On a home, figure it by taking the sale value of your home and then subtracting the amount you still owe on your mortgage and the amount it would cost to make the sale. For example, if your home could be sold for $40,000 and you owe $20,000 on your mortgage and it would cost $2,000 to sell (realtor's commissions, etc.), then your equity is $18,000.

Judgment Proof—This means that you simply don't have to worry about debts because you have nothing that anyone can legally take away from you. If after reading this book you conclude that you are judgment proof, you can relax. A family would be judgment proof if, for example, they live on social security, have less than $1,000 deposited in a savings and loan association or $1500 in a credit union, have an old inexpensive car and a house with an equity of less than $45,000. You will learn a great deal about being judgment proof as we go along. At this point we just want you to be familiar with the term. IMPORTANT: It is possible to be judgment proof now, but have to pay judgments including attorney fees and court costs later on. This would be the case in the example given above if the family was given or had inherited money or property or the head of the family went back to work.

Personal Property—All property other than land and buildings attached to land. Cars, bank accounts, wages, furniture, mobile homes, insurance policies, etc., are all personal property.

Promissory Note—A written promise to pay.

Real Property—Land and the buildings built on the land. Your home is real property.

---

* If the principal parties to a contract change the terms of the agreement without the approval of the co-signer, he or she is no longer responsible. Also, any defenses that a principal to a contract may raise may be raised by the co-signer. See Cal. Civil Code Section 2819; *Wexler v. McLucas* 48 CA3 Supp. 9 (1975).

CHAPTER 2

DEBTS YOU FEEL
YOU DON'T OWE

This book deals primarily with being over your head with debts you feel you legally owe. We do not spend time on situations where you feel you have been screwed over by dishonest salesmen or creditors. This is the subject for a book on consumer rights. But we will review a great deal of this area here and outline several helpful approaches.

Often disputes arise between the buyer and seller of goods and services over such things as unexplained credit charges, excessive interest, shoddy work or merchandise, failure to perform work or supply goods in the time promised, and the delivery of goods or services different from those promised. Sometimes these disputes involve simple misunderstandings between honest people and sometimes they involve misrepresentations or outright fraud. Your first job is to get your head clear as to exactly what sort of situation you face. Ask yourself these questions:

a) Am I dealing with a reputable person or corporation?

b) Have I done anything to contribute to the misunderstanding?

c) Is there a reasonable chance that some sort of compromise can be worked out?

Don't let your own anger, no matter how justifiable, blind you to the situation you face and the best way to deal with it.

17

WARRANTIES! You are entitled to rely on any written warranty that comes with a product. You should also know that under state law (Civil Code Section 1791.1), many products (mostly machines, appliances, motor vehicles, mobile homes, etc.) are covered by an implied warranty of "merchantability" and "fitness." This means that the product is reasonably workable (isn't defective) and, if the seller knows what the buyer plans to use it for, will reasonably fill this need. The period of time for which an implied warranty is good is the same as any written warranty that comes with a product if there is one (but in no case is shorter than 60 days). If there is no written warranty stating a shorter period than one year, the implied warranty period is one year. If an express or implied warranty is breached, the consumer may be entitled to a refund or damages. For details, see the California Civil Code Sections 1791 to 1797.5. Products clearly marked "as is" or "with all defects" are not covered by warranty.

NOTE—California law grants people a three-day cooling off period on door-to-door sales if the amount involved is $25 or more. Notify the creditor (use certified mail) in writing before midnight of the third business day after signing the contract that you wish to cancel and they must return your money within 10 days, Civil Code Section 1689.5 et seq.

A. IF YOU HAVE BEEN DEFRAUDED

If you believe you have been cheated, you should immediately let several county, state, and federal agencies know about it. They may be able to help you directly and at least will have the information necessary for moving against the crooks. Law enforcement in the consumer fraud area is not as good as it should be, but it's vastly better than it was a few years ago. Once you decide that fraud may be involved, the faster you move the better. Do not pay anything in a situation where you believe you have been swindled. Nofity immediately:

a) The District Attorney in the county in which you live. Call them and ask for a person who handles consumer fraud complaints. They will send you a complaint form.

b) State of California, Office of the Attorney General, Consumer Fraud Unit, 555 Capitol Mall, Sacramento, California 95814 or call the Public Inquiry Unit on the toll-free number [800] 952-5225. (Your complaint will be routed through this office to the deputy attorney general most familiar with your area of concern. You can get a complaint form by calling the Attorney

General in Los Angeles, San Francisco, or Sacramento.)

c) The Federal Trade Commission, Room 13209 Federal Building, 11000 Wilshire Boulevard, Los Angeles, California 90024 OR 450 Golden Gate Avenue, Box 36005, San Francisco, California 94102. (It's best to call first and get a complaint form.)

d) There are dozens of state and federal offices that are geared to handling individual areas of concern. For example, there is one office that you complain to about optometrists and another about osteopaths. See your metropolitan phone book white pages under Consumer Complaint and Protection Coordinators and you will find many listings,* or call [916] 445-1254.

IMPORTANT—Keep all contracts, letters, guarantees, etc., that relate to the dispute and try to get all promises in writing. Business people keep records or they don't stay in business long. To protect yourself, so must you. Be sure to keep copies of letters you send to the creditors.

B. MISUNDERSTANDINGS BETWEEN BUYER AND SELLER

All too often services are not performed properly or goods turn out to be defective or are not delivered on time. We are all familiar with the car that falls apart a few days after purchase, the roof that leaks more after repair than before, and the merchandise that shows up six months after you don't want it any more.

1. When You Have Paid

If you have paid for goods or services before you learn they are somehow not right, you should first ask the dealer to fix the problem. Be sure to consult any guarantee or written contract to see if these help you. If you have lost these documents, request copies from the seller of the goods. If after complaining to those concerned about the problem, no fair compromise is agreed to, you will need to assert yourself. Remember, some creditors will promise you the moon and deliver nothing. Don't let anyone jive you too long. Your first step is to write a letter setting out your contentions in detail. Send a copy of the letter to any state, federal or local agency interested in the area and let the creditor know you have done so. This puts the seller on notice that you

---

* The State of California also publishes an extremely helpful pamphlet, *The Compleat California Consumer Catalogue*. It's available at many state offices including the Department of Motor Vehicles.

```
                                             315 Main Street
                                             Oakland, California
                                             March 18, 19___


Over the Rainbow Used Chariots
331 10th Street
Berkeley, California

     On March 10, 19___ I purchased a 1980 Chevrolet from your company, and
paid you $3,000 cash.  You specifically told me that the car had only been
driven 20,000 miles, that it had been completely checked by your mechanics
and that, to the best of your knowledge, the car was in good shape.

     On March 14, 19___ I drove the car to Stockton, California.  While there,
the entire tail pipe and muffler fell off and the car started smoking.  On
investigation, I found that the tail pipe clamps were missing and that the
tail pipe itself was secured to the bottom of the car with a piece of twisted
wire.  I also discovered that the engine contained a heavy grade of truck
oil, apparently so that the existence of two badly burned valves would not
be noticed.

     Because the car was unsafe to drive back to Berkeley, I took it to the
Chevrolet dealership in Stockton.  They made the necessary repairs and charged
me $802.00.  I enclose a photocopy of the bill.  When I returned to Berkeley,
I called your office and asked you to pay this amount.  In that conversation,
you treated me rudely and said you would not pay me a penny.

     Please send me the $802.00 immediately.  If I don't hear from you by
March 23, I plan to take legal action.


                                        Very truly yours,


                                        Helen West

copies sent to:
  1. District Investigator, Department of Motor Vehicles
     (address of nearest Motor Vehicles Office)
  2. Consumer Fraud Section, District Attorney of _____
        County.
  3. State of California, Department of Consumer Affairs
```

are serious. It is also a good idea to contact the original manufacturer of a product if your dispute is with a middleman. General Electric, for example, has a real interest in seeing that a
hardware store which sells their toasters treats people honestly.

If conversation and a letter or two fail, you have to get serious, or drop the matter. Only you can decide whether the dispute is worth the trouble of continuing to hassle.* Assuming you decide to persevere, it may be wise to see a lawyer at this stage if your claim is for a lot of money. He or she may be able to write a letter or make a phone call that will solve the problem. Unfortunately, there is often a big psychological difference between getting a letter from you and getting one on legal letterhead (see Chapter 3). If a large amount of money is involved you may want to retain a lawyer to start a lawsuit in Municipal (up to $15,000) Court or Superior (over $15,000) Court. But be sure you understand clearly how much this will cost before you get involved in it. Consider too, that lawsuits can be lost and that it is sometimes easier to win the suit than it is to collect on the judgment.

You may also want to consider suing in Small Claims Court. No lawyers are allowed in this court and you can sue for any amount up to $750.** If your claim is greater than this amount, you will either have to waive the excess or not use Small Claims Court. The rules for Small Claims Court are contained in California Code of Civil Procedure Section 116-117.20. This book is available at *most* public libraries and at all county law libraries. Also you will want to see *Everybody's Guide to Small Claims Court,* Warner, Nolo Press, $7.95 (see notice at back of this book).

To sue in Small Claims Court go to your local municipal courthouse and find the Clerk of the Small Claims Court. The clerk is required by law to fill out a complaint form for you if you so request. On the form you state how much money you are owed and the reason for the claim. After you file the form with the clerk, the clerk will advise you as to how to best serve the defendant with an order for him to appear in court on a certain date and time. Often, but not always, service can be accomplished by mail.

---

* You may get some good advice at this point from others who have had a similar problem. In Northern California call S.F. Consumer Action, [415] 626-4032 or the Bureau of Automotive Repair, toll-free, between 7:30 and 5:30, [800] 942-5210.

** We favor legislation to greatly increase this amount. People should be able to handle their own disputes without lawyers at least up to $5,000 (in many situations $10,000 would be reasonable).

Your court date will be not more than 40 days nor less than 10 days if the defendant lives within your county, or not more than 70 days nor less than 30 days if he lives in another county.

Trials in Small Claims Court are informal. It doesn't help a bit to have watched Perry Mason, or the other T.V. lawyers, since there are no lawyers or rules of evidence. Simply bring all records including photographs, letters, contracts, etc., that you believe back up your case. Also bring all witnesses who have first hand information about the facts in dispute. Don't be afraid of the court. Go down a few days before and watch a few cases if you are at all nervous. It's a very simple procedure and you will see that people do best when they tell their story briefly and logically and present witnesses and documents in an orderly way. If you tell the judge a great long story, he will get bored and possibly irritated. Remember, he hears many cases every day and will not be particularly excited about yours. The more long-winded you are, the more likely he is to start thinking about his lunch.

2. When You Have Not Paid

Sometime in elementary school you probably heard the expression "possession is nine-tenths of the law." After more years of law school than we care to think about, we can tell you that this grade school wisdom is very often right on. If you are unhappy about goods or services you ordered and have a legitimate reason for your concern, don't pay. You are in possession of the money and no one can get it from you short of a law suit. Law suits are unpleasant and expensive to start. It is in the seller's interest to make any reasonable compromise with you in order to get paid and get the matter settled without court action.

Should you receive a bill which you believe to be unfair either in whole or part, it is wise to call or write the company involved.

IMPORTANT—If you believe that you owe part, but not all of a bill it is often psychologically wise to send a check or money

5377 Sweet William St.
Mendocino, California
May 10, 19___

Honest John Paints
1515 Olive St.
Sacramento, California

Dear Honest John:

I received your bill today for $750 for painting my living room.
I do not feel that I owe you this amount.

It is true that we signed a contract saying that you would get
$750 for the work, but it was clearly understood that you were to do
the work in a careful, businesslike way. Instead, you sent out an
inexperienced painter who did the following:

1. Dripped paint on a rug valued at $400, ruining it;

2. Left paint streaks on windows which took me five hours to
clean off with a razor blade.

I am willing to pay you $350 for the work done, and will send you
a check for that amount as soon as you send me a corrected bill.

Very truly yours,

Roz Bindman

---

180 Phoenix Avenue
Belmont, California
May 10, 19___

Honest John Paints
1515 Olive Street
Sacramento, California

Dear Honest John:

Today I received a bill for $750 for painting. I have no inten-
tion of paying it, as the work was not done.

On April 14, 19___ you sent an untrained painter to my house. In
the first hour he spilled paint on my rug, started to apply enamel
paint meant for woodwork to the ceiling, and kicked my dog. I requested that he leave, and he did so.

If you persist in bothering me about this bill, I plan to file a
formal complaint with the consumer fraud section of the District Attorney's office and will consult an attorney concerning legal rights as
far as suing you for damages.

Very truly yours,

Sally Elizabeth Pooler

order for the amount you feel you owe, along with your letter explaining your position. If you do this, write on the back of the check, where the endorsement would normally go, a statement that cashing the check constitutes full settlement of all debts between you and the other party. In the first letter above, the back of your check would look like this:

Cashing of this check by
Honest John Paints
constitutes full satisfaction
of all debts owed to them
by Roz Bindman.

If you can't work out any sort of compromise and you keep being hassled by a creditor, it is important that you pay attention to what is happening and protect yourself. You will want to do one or more of the following:

a) Complain to at least one of the agencies listed in section A of this chapter or in the Consumer Complaint and Protection Coordinators section of your metropolitan phone book white pages.

b) If a lot of money is involved, consider consulting an attorney for advice and perhaps for help in compromising the claim (see Chapter 3).

c) Fight any lawsuit that is filed against you.

C. WHAT IF A 3rd PARTY OWNS YOUR DEBT?

It often happens that the original person with whom you deal (say a furniture dealer) sells your debt obligation to a third party (say a bank). You now owe monthly payments to the bank. But what happens if something major goes wrong with the furniture? Can you raise the claim against the bank and perhaps refuse to pay them until some fair adjustment is made? The answer used to be generally "No", under a particularly unfair to consumers legal doctrine known as "Holder in Due Course." This has recently been changed and the answer is now "Yes", you can normally assert claims against third parties. As we stated earlier a good general rule is not to pay for goods or services that are defective until some adjustment is made. Be sure to notify everyone involved in the dispute (manufacturer, seller, finance company or bank, etc.) of why you are refusing to pay. Keep carbon or xerox copies of all communications.

D. IF YOU ARE SUED

Please turn to chapter 8 which contains a full discussion of law suits and how to protect yourself.

CHAPTER 3

LAWYERS AND CREDIT COUNSELLORS

A. LAWYERS—DOING YOUR OWN RESEARCH

Within the past decade people have become more sophisticated in dealing with legal problems. Many people now take their own case to court - not only to Small Claims Court but also Municipal and Superior Court. See Chapter 8. But whether you intend to handle your own case or not, you should know all the law which applies to it. This book is your beginning. But sometimes your situation will not be fully covered. So where do you go next?

Rather than run right to a lawyer, you may want to research the problem yourself. Researching the law is actually easier than you might think. The law books are, for the most part, logically indexed, and complement each other. It shouldn't take you long figuring out how to search through the Civil Code (or any other statute) or look up and read a case. Law, though cloaked in mystery, is actually pretty easy to unveil.

Law materials are available in law school libraries and county law libraries which are located in the principal county courthouses. The county law libraries are open to the public; law school libraries may have some restrictions; you'll have to check. City public libraries and college libraries also have some law materials, but are not as complete.

A useful text written expressly for consumers (as well as law students) on how to use law materials is *Gilberts: Legal Research,* by Peter Jan Honigsberg (available at any law bookstore). Nolo Press also publishes a legal research book called *How to Find and Understand the Law,* by Steve Elias.

1. What Lawyers Can Do For You

There are four basic ways a lawyer can help you:

a. Consultation and Advice: The lawyer can listen to the details of your situation, analyze it for you, and advise you on your position and best plan of action. Ideally he will give you more than just conclusions—he can educate you about your whole situation and tell you all the alternatives available from which you can make your own choices. This kind of service is the least expensive since it only involves an office call and a little time. A charge of more than $40 for a consultation might be considered excessive. Find out the fee **before** you go in.

b. Negotiation: The lawyer can use his special talents, knowledge and experience to help you negotiate with the creditor to your best advantage. In case of serious problems, he can do this more successfully than you, especially if you are at odds with the creditor, or if your creditor has an attorney. Without spending much of his own time, he can often accomplish a lot through a letter or phone call. Receiving a message on an attorney's letterhead is, in itself, often very sobering to a creditor. He knows you mean business. A lawyer can sometimes possess considerable skill as a negotiator. Also, if bad turns to worse, a lawyer can often bluff by threatening legal action. You can then decide at a later time whether to actually pursue it. In trying to compromise debts (see chapter 7) a lawyer can be particularly helpful as the creditor knows that he is the person who would file a bankruptcy.

c. Law Suits: In some rare instances your case should go to court. Having a lawyer handle a court case is very expensive, and only rarely warranted. If the creditor sues you on a debt that you don't feel you owe, it is a little more likely that you will need a lawyer's help.

d. Bankruptcy: It is not difficult to do your own bankruptcy but you may want to check your paperwork with a lawyer or someone else who is thoroughly familiar with bankruptcy law and procedure if you feel at all unsure (see Chapter 18). With a little shopping around you should be able to find a lawyer who will look over your papers for $50–$100. If you make a mistake in a bankruptcy (i.e., don't list all of your debts), it can be impossible to fix later.

Whenever you think of using a lawyer, keep in mind this view of clients that is held by a lawyer-friend of ours: He imagines a man who has built a shack on some old railroad tracks in a high mountain valley. One day, when the man puts his ear to the track, he hears a distant vibration. A few days later he can hear the sound of a train rumbling on the warm breeze that blows up the canyon, and soon the sound is distinctly audible. At this point he can begin to see the smoke of the engine, and not much later the train is running down on him, spitting fire and belching smoke. When the thing is fifty yards away, the man picks up his phone, calls his lawyer and asks him to get an injunction to stop the railroad company. What we mean to say is . . . if you decide to use a lawyer, don't wait until it's too late.

2. When Do You Need A Lawyer?

There is no simple answer to the question of when you need a lawyer. This is because there are many possible areas of dispute between creditor and debtor, and many levels of debtor ability to deal with problems. Throughout this book we will suggest times when the advice or other services of an attorney would be useful, but here are a few general pointers:

a) If you are sued for a lot of money that you don't feel you owe (if you have a written contract or sales agreement with a creditor which allows the creditor attorneys fees, California law says that the debtor is also entitled to recover attorneys fees should he win a law suit based on the terms of the agreement).

b) To check bankruptcy papers (see Chapter 18);

c) If, after reading this book, you feel that you want assistance in negotiating a settlement with the creditor;

d) If your wages are attached and you feel you need help after reading chapter 10;

e) If, after reading this book, you feel you still don't understand what you are up against.

3. Finding A Lawyer

Finding a lawyer who charges reasonable prices and whom you feel can be trusted is not always an easy task. There is always the realistic fear that by just picking a name out of the telephone book you may get someone unsympathetic or perhaps an attorney who will charge too much. You should realize that you are not the only one who feels a little scared and intimidated. Here are some suggestions:

a. Legal Aid: If you are poor, you may qualify for free help from your legal aid office (often called legal services or legal assistance). Check your yellow pages under Attorneys for their location, or ask your county clerk.

b. Group Legal Practices: A new but rapidly growing aspect of California law practice is the Group Legal Practice program. Many groups, including unions, employers and consumer action groups, are offering plans to their members whereby they can get legal assistance for rates which are substantially lower than offered by most private practitioners. Some of these plans are good, some mediocre, and a few are not worth much, but most are better than nothing. In the San Francisco Bay region, a good plan is offered through the Consumers Cooperative of Berkeley, Inc. In the L. A. area the Jacoby & Meyers Legal Clinics do a good job. Because the group practice area of the law is changing so rapidly, we can't give you a statewide list of group legal plans. If you contact one of the above groups, however, they may be able to help you find a good group practice plan in your area.

c. Private Attorneys: If you don't know an attorney that can be trusted and can't get a reliable recommendation from a friend, you have a problem. While you might be lucky and randomly pick an attorney who matches your needs perfectly, you might just as easily wind up paying too much for too little. Here are some suggestions that should make your search a little easier:

• Referral panels set up by local bar associations. Lawyers are initially screened on their expertise in consumer matters. There is usually a small fee for an initial consultation. You may get a good referral from these panels, but be sure to question the lawyer whose name you are given about his or her qualifications and sympathy to your rights as a consumer. As a rule, panels of the National Lawyers Guild refer you to good, inexpensive, and sympathetic lawyers.

• Check with a local consumer organization to see if they can recommend someone;

• Consult the ads in the classified section of the newspaper under Attorneys. This will give you a good idea as to price and range of services offered.

• Shop around by calling different law offices and stating your problem. Ask them how much it would cost for a visit. Try to talk to a lawyer personally to attempt to get an idea of how friendly and sympathetic he is to your concerns. Offices that use the word "Legal Clinic" in their title often specialize in the mass production of simple types of cases (bankruptcy, divorce, debt problems, etc.) at reasonable prices.

• Remember, lawyers whose offices and life styles are reasonably simple are more likely to help you for less money than lawyers who feel naked unless wearing a $500 outfit. You should be able to find an attorney willing to discuss your problems for $35–$50.

B. DEBT CONSOLIDATION SERVICES

Much of what passes for credit counselling is no more than a front for loan sharking. The idea is to lend you more money at outrageous rates (up to 30% per year), rather than help you get out of debt. Debt consolidation loans definitely fall into this category. These loans are normally made by finance or thrift companies, whose consolidation loan practices should, in our opinion, be outlawed by State Law. Consolidation outfits put all your debts together and charge only one payment—one impossible payment. If you are already in the hole don't try to get out by digging deeper.

C. CREDIT COUNSELING

There is one counseling service in the state that we can recommend. It is Consumer Credit Counselors. We include a list of their offices below. C.C.C. is a nonprofit organization set up and sponsored by large respectable creditors such as department stores, banks, etc. They want you to pay your debts and feel that they will benefit in the long run by giving you counseling as to how to do it. They hate the notion of bankruptcy, as all creditors do. If you are interested in bankruptcy, read chapter 18 and stay away from C.C.C. However, if you feel you can pay your debts with a little time and are willing to work out a detailed budget and stick to it, C.C.C. can help you. They have a plan allowing you to make one or two payments per month to them. They then divide the money among your creditors, after getting the creditors to agree to extend your time to pay. Because C.C.C. is set up by the creditors, it has a lot of influence. It can stop wage attachments and often get interest and late charges wiped out altogether. The only charge for this service is 6½% of the money paid creditors each month or $12, whichever is less. There is no charge at all for counseling, making a budget, etc.

You can get free information about the services offered by contacting any of the following offices:

C.C.C. of San Francisco
  and the Peninsula
1429 Market Street
San Francisco, CA 94103
[415] 431-0510

C.C.C. of Santa Clara Valley
816 N. 1st Street, Suite K
San Jose, CA 95108
[408] 286-8826

C.C.C. of Sacramento
1815 J Street
Sacramento, CA 95814
[916] 444-0740

C.C.C. of San Diego
P.O. Box 2131
San Diego, CA 92112
[714] 234-4118

C.C.C. of Los Angeles
650 S. Spring St.
Los Angeles, CA 90014
[213] 624-1561

C.C.C. of Orange County
1616 E. 4th Street, Suite D
Santa Ana, CA 92701
[714] 547-8281

C.C.C. of Kern County
1304 Chester
Bakersfield, CA 93301
[805] 324-9628

C.C.C. of The East Bay
1212 Broadway, Suite 706
Oakland, CA 94612
[415] 832-7555

C.C.C. of Twin Cities
729 "D" Street
Marysville, CA 95901
[916] 743-1785

C.C.C. of Fresno
2135 Fresno Street, Room 213
Fresno, CA 93721
[209] 233-6221

C.C.C. of Inland Empire
(San Bernardino)
3679 Arlington Ave., Suite E
Riverside, CA 92506
[714] 781-0114

C.C.C. of Ventura County
2122 Thompson Blvd.
Ventura, CA 93001
[805] 648-1352

C.C.C. of Pleasant Hill
85 Cleveland
Pleasant Hill, CA 94523
[415] 832-7555

C.C.C. of Marin County
(see San Francisco)

C.C.C. of Stockton
343 E. Main, Room 629
Stockton, CA 95202
[209] 464-8319

C.C.C. of North Valley
1525 Pine Street, #12
Redding, CA 96099
[916] 244-9626

C.C.C. of Sonoma
[707] 527-9221

33

CHAPTER 4

CREDIT BUREAUS AND DISCRIMINATION IN CREDIT

I. CREDIT BUREAUS

Credit bureaus are a direct result of our insane credit system. The credit system expands because creditors thrust more and more credit into people's lives. But with each additional person using credit, the paranoia of the creditor in not collecting on the debt likewise increases. To protect themselves from their self-created paranoia, creditors keep intensifying their investigations of the people to whom they are lending money. The result— more credit bureaus. Sounds a bit crazy, huh.

A. WHAT ARE THEY?

Credit bureaus are profit making companies which are usually in partnership with collection agencies or are in fact collection agencies themselves. The bureaus survive by providing information on a person's credit reputation to other collection agencies, and to all kinds of creditors like finance companies, department stores, car dealers, landlords, etc. If the bureau has no information on a person, it can't very well charge for providing a service. What that means is they're always out there digging.

Credit bureaus are known officially as Consumer Credit Reporting Agencies. There are also Investigative Consumer Reporting Agencies which report on your personal life. Most outfits are made up of both types of agencies, having all the information on you right on hand.

B. WHAT "SERVICES" DO THEY PROVIDE?

It is their business to gather as much data as possible on **everyone** including **you.** With that information, they can provide their nasty service to any creditor who wants to know about you.

The frightening aspect of these bureaus is that they can gather information that goes beyond mere credit information. Under the law, they can collect data on your personal life such as whether you are divorced, separated, have been arrested or convicted of a crime or failed to pay a traffic fine. The law specifically provides for investigative information on your "general reputation," "personal characteristics" and "mode of living." Obviously these words could mean anything and possibly they may only be limited by the imagination of the credit bureau people.*

Credit bureaus also keep "locate" lists. If, for example, ABC creditor has trouble finding Roger who skipped out on one of their loans, they can give his name to the credit bureau and ask them to put his name on "locate." Then each time a name is called in for some other reason, whether for a credit check by another creditor or perhaps by the person himself who wants to see his file, or whatever, it is checked against this list. If Roger's name comes up, they call ABC creditor and tell him that Roger has been found and has given 1 Blue Street, Pasadena, California, as his address. Pretty sneaky, don't you think?

C. HOW THE BUREAU WORKS

Let's see what happens when someone, let's call him Roger Owens, buys a car on credit.

Roger Owens goes to Trust-in-Man Autos and finds a 1970

---

* The "imagination" of credit bureau people often seems to tread on lawlessness. Instead of accurately checking sources on personal information it received, one of the largest credit bureaus in the country was recently found to be faking investigations and verifications. Even more outrageously, it bribed hospital employees, policemen, medical computer employees and anyone else it could in order to get official records of people for its files. All this was soundly illegal, not to say a ghastly invasion of privacy. See Petrocelli, William, *Law Profile, How to Avoid the Privacy Invaders*, 1981.

Volvo with 80,000 original miles. He'd like to buy it and the salesman offers to sell it for the fine price of $1,000. Roger bites, and now the salesman needs to check his credit. For even though Roger must put $300 down, Trust-in-Man Autos must assure itself that Roger will be able to pay the remaining $700 plus interest at 22% a year.

The salesman calls Credit Bureau Inc. (C.B.I.), one of the largest credit bureaus, to see what they have on Roger.* The person who answers will type on a computer terminal Roger's name, his social security number, his current address, former employment, his wife's name, her employment and perhaps also her social security number. All this information then appears before that person on the screen. The computer will digest the information and soon come up with a "file" on Roger. It will contain whatever credit information it has on him including any bankruptcies within the last 14 years, law suits and judgments, tax liens, all within the last 7 years. If he's had trouble getting credit at another place, it may be written down here, as would any repayment difficulties he may have had. There is a rating system from 1 to 9 depending on whether he usually pays within 30 days (rating 1), 60 days (rating 2), 90 days (rating 3), etc., up to rating 8 where the item has been repossessed and rating 9 where the account is labelled "skip" and is referred for collection.** (See chart.)

If all the information that the salesman receives is sufficient for him, he will use it to make a decision as to whether Trust-in-Man Autos can "afford" to take the chance of financing Roger on the car.

Now what if Roger recently moved here from Alburquerque. There may not be a record of him in the local credit bureau office. If that happens, the credit bureau will do two things. It will call its office in Alburquerque (if it has one) to see what they have on him. And it will start a new file on him, so if any other creditor needs to know about Roger, the bureau will be able to supply some information.

---

* Some bureaus are small and local, but others are national in scope. Equifax, a credit and investigative reporting agency, for example, has approximately 1800 offices coast to coast and employs a small army of investigators.

** Rating systems and codes vary, but most are roughly like this example.

IMPORTANT: HOW LONG CAN A CREDIT BUREAU KEEP AN ITEM IN YOUR FILE ?

The credit bureau is permitted to keep the following credit information in your file (Civil Code Section 1785.13):

1. Bankruptcies which happened less than 10 years ago (see 15 U.S.C. Section 1681C).

2. Lawsuits and paid judgments which happened less than seven years ago.

3. Unpaid judgments which happened less than ten years ago.

4. Any other adverse information which is less than seven years old.

5. Records of arrests and convictions up to seven years ago. However, if you were arrested but never convicted, the item must be removed immediately.

Don't trust the credit bureau to automatically remove the information once the time period has passed. Review your file. Also, if the time period hasn't lapsed on an item, but you disagree with the way the information is presented in your file, you can dispute it. See H(3) below.

D. WANT TO KEEP YOUR NAME OUT OF CREDIT BUREAUS?

The above example should give you some clues on what to do if you don't want credit bureaus to have information about you. You see, the credit bureau finds you only when you find them. And you may find them each time you apply for credit, or loans, or employment, or even an apartment. Obviously, at some time you will have to rent a place, or look for a job. But not every landlord or employer checks with a credit bureau. If possible, don't deal with people who want to do a check on you. For if the bureau has nothing on you when the creditor calls, it will start a file then. Always pay in cash. You'll be happier in the long run and less paranoid.

Credit bureaus also find out about you if you file bankruptcy, or have lawsuits and judgments* brought against you. These facts surface because people from the bureau check local court records each week. But they usually only check local court records so if you move to a new town, they won't necessarily know what your credit standing was before, unless you tell them.

---

* Credit bureaus will seldom include that you have paid the judgment or won the lawsuit.

E. WHAT IF YOU HAVE NO FILE?

If the credit bureau has no file on you, some creditors might figure you're a good risk, especially if the reason there is no file is that you had no reason to get credit before. But most creditors will not figure you're a good risk because you have not demonstrated that you can buy on credit and pay on time. To establish good credit, you might consider getting a department store credit card, purchasing a few small items, and paying for them as soon as you receive the bill.

F. WANT TO KNOW WHAT IS IN YOUR FILE?

Under California law, you have the right to see and copy your files. All you have to do is establish proper identification and usually pay a small fee of around $4 or $5. (Civ. Code 1785.10 and 1786.10.)

G. WHICH CREDIT BUREAU SHOULD YOU CONTACT?

You can find a listing of credit bureaus in your area by looking up "Credit Reporting Agencies" in the yellow pages of your phone book.

There are often 3 or 4 credit bureaus in a locale, especially in major metropolitan areas. Some will be larger than others and one will probably contain more information on you than another. The largest in California are T.R.W., C.B.I. (Credit Bureau, Inc.), and Trans Union Credit.

Some bureaus may charge you less or perhaps no fee at all to see your file. If you are not afraid of giving your name to a credit bureau, call a few of them and see whether they have a file on you and if so whether there is a charge for you to check it out.

Of course, if you've received a letter saying that your credit has been denied because of information in your file at a certain credit bureau, then that's where you will want to check. Under the law, if you were denied credit or you have been charged a greater than normal interest rate because of information in your file, you are permitted to see your file without charge if you ask to see it within 30 days. (The person who received the bureau report must tell you and give you the name of the bureau.)

H. YOU'VE FOUND A CREDIT BUREAU: WHAT NEXT?

1. Call The Bureau

Call the bureau and ask to see your file. They may establish your identity right then over the phone and tell you what's in your file. More likely, though, they'll either send you an identification form to fill out (and maybe give you a "code" number to use) or ask you to call back after they've searched for your file. *

If they want you to fill out a form, be careful. There are some bureaus that use their right to ask for identification to get even more information about you for their records. (After all,

---

* A married or divorced woman can now use her birth given name and not have to refer to her husband or former husband's name to gain access to her file. See "B" of part II of this chapter.

the more information they have on you, the more they will have to sell to collection agencies and creditors who want it.) Answer only those questions which will establish your identity, like giving your name, social security number, address and perhaps a previous address. One credit bureau asks for five years of previous addresses. There is usually no need to give them all that information. If a credit bureau refuses you the right to see your file after you provide "proper identification" and pay the fee, complain to one of the State Attorney General's offices listed at the end of this chapter.

In our experience we found that one bureau which reads files over the phone told us the day we called that the computer wasn't working and that we should call back. We did. And did. And did. And did. Each time all we got was a pleasant greeting and a hold. It took us 3 days to get back through to the woman with whom we were to discuss our file.

Another problem with calling by phone is that if they do read your file over the phone to you, you can never be certain that they are telling you everything in it.

2. Seeing Your Computer Printout

Some offices will send you a computer printout of your file. Others will allow you to visit their offices to review the printout on the premises with a staff member. It doesn't really make that much difference, although if you review your statement in the company of a bureau employee, you can immediately receive clarification of all the unintelligible code numbers and symbols used. If you read it at home, you may find that the explanations printed on the bottom or reverse side of your statement are as indecipherable as the symbols they are interpreting. Calling up for clarification can be a bureaucratic nightmare.

If you visit the office you are permitted to bring someone else with you. This is probably a good idea. Your friend can act as a witness if the bureau gives you any trouble in requiring you to fill out unnecessary forms, or makes you rush through the file not giving you sufficient time to go over it carefully and ask questions.

The credit bureau must allow you to see all the information they have in your file (except medical information) at the time of your request, the sources of the information they have on you, the names of the people who have received information from your file within the last six months, and within the last two years if the information was given to an employer or potential employer of yours.

IMPORTANT—Don't let them skip over anything.

3. What If you Disagree
With Something In Your File?

You have the right to dispute any item of information in your file. Bureaus very often have inaccurate or misleading material in their files. If you see something that isn't true or is inaccurate, complain. Under the law, the bureau is required to reinvestigate the matter. If you are right or if the information can no longer be verified, the bureau must remove that information. Our experience has been that if you dispute an item, they'll often remove it or state it the way you feel it should be. Credit bureaus cannot afford the time and the staff to go out and recheck information on individual files.

If the bureau verifies the information and you still disagree with it, you are entitled to write a statement up to 100 words on the disagreement. The bureau people must include it in your file. (Civil Code Section 1785.16.)

a. Writing Your Statement

The law requires that the credit bureau people assist you with the writing of your statement, if you ask them for their help. However, they may use pre-packaged statements or not help you say exactly what you want.

If you would rather write it yourself, ask the friend who has come with you to help. You can also wait until you get home to write it and bring it back another day.

On the next page are a couple of different kinds of statements to give you an idea on how to write one.

STATEMENT 1

Your records showing that I was not making payments on time to Rip-Off Furniture Store in Fresno are misleading. I stopped making payments to them only after the new sofa I purchased for $400 fell apart 3 months after I bought it. I decided that I would not pay any longer for such junk. After a few months went by, they contacted me and we settled the remainder of the account by my agreeing to give them only $50 more and to pay for the repair work myself. The account is closed and I owe them nothing.

Suzanne Porter

STATEMENT 2

Your records show that I am unemployed. That is incorrect. I am self-employed as a cabinet maker and carpenter. I work out of my home and take orders from people who are referred to me through various sources. My work is known in the community and that is how I earn my living.

Denny Porter

b. After A Change Is Made In Your File

If the bureau revises certain information in your file, or if you write a statement for inclusion in your file, the bureau must comply in the following manner: If you filed a statement, they must read your statement or give a summary of it to anyone to whom they give the report. The bureau must also notify any person who has received a report on you within 6 months (or 2 years if it involves employment) of the statement you have made, should you request the bureau to notify them. (There may be an additional charge for this.) BUT YOU HAVE TO

DEMAND THAT IT BE DONE. You should also consider sending a copy of any such information yourself to important creditors and the like to be sure they receive it.

c. Preventive Tips

Applications for jobs, insurance, or apartments may spur investigative consumer reports, so be sure to correct any inaccuracies *before* making the application.

I. HAVE A GRIPE ABOUT THE CREDIT BUREAU?

If you feel that the credit bureau or the person or creditor that received a report on you misused the report or otherwise failed to comply with the law, you should make a complaint to the State Attorney General's office which covers your area. There is one in Sacramento, San Francisco, Los Angeles, and San Diego. Their addresses and phone numbers are listed below. If you call these offices, they will send you a complaint form to fill out and return. If you would rather not call, you can send a letter which they will accept as a substitute for a complaint form. If you write a letter include, if possible, the name of the company, its address, the name of the person you dealt with, the nature of the problem, any dates, and copies of any documents or letters that pertain to the problem.

A sample letter appears on the following page.

1. Here is a list of Attorney General's Offices in the state. Contact the one nearest to you.

LOS ANGELES:
Tishman Building
3580 Wilshire Blvd.
Los Angeles, CA 90010
(213) 736-2304

SAN FRANCISCO
350 McAllister, Rm. 6000
San Francisco, CA 94102
(415) 557-2544

615 Cloisters
San Diego, California
April 2, 19____

Consumer Complaint Division
State Attorney General's Office
1350 Front Street
Room 5006
San Diego, California 92101

Dear Sir:

I wish to make the following complaint concerning Sneaky Credit Bureau, 503 Grand Avenue, San Diego.

On March 29, 19____I went down to Sneaky Credit Bureau to see my file. I paid $4.00 and waited until someone was available to help me. Finally, a Mrs. Jones came out and took me back with her to a small room. There she pulled out my file and started going through it.

However, she refused to show me certain pages and when I asked her why, she said she didn't have to show these to me. She wouldn't tell me what kind of information was in it, but just ignored my question.

She also went through the file very quickly and wouldn't give me any time to stop and ask questions. When I asked her to check on a statement in the file that I felt was inaccurate, she told me not to worry about it.

Kindly investigate this matter and inform me of the results.

Very truly yours,

Georgann Stewart

SAN DIEGO:
110 W. "A" Street
San Diego, CA 92101
(714) 236-7351

SACRAMENTO:
555 Capitol Mall, Suite 550
Sacramento, CA 95814
(916) 445-9555

2. You can also contact your local District Attorney's office if they have a consumer complaint division.

3. If the credit bureau is associated with a collection agency (and most of them are), you can also contact the California Collection Agency Licensing Bureau at 1430 Howe Avenue in Sacramento ([916] 920-6424) and make a complaint.

But probably your best results will be the Attorney General's Office.

If you were seriously screwed over by the credit bureau as, for example, they repeatedly gave out false information on you after you corrected it, you may also want to see a lawyer. The law allows you to bring suit against credit bureaus in certain instances.

Under California law, you can sue credit bureaus for actual damages including court costs, loss of wages, attorney's fees, and, when applicable, pain and suffering. In the case of a willful violation you can recover punitive damages of $100 to $5000 (Civil Code Section 1785.31). You can bring your case yourself in Small Claims Court (see Chapter 8).

II. DISCRIMINATION IN CREDIT

The Federal Equal Credit Opportunity Act prohibits discrimination on the basis of race, color, religion, national origin, sex, marital status, age and being on public assistance. The law allows the creditor in certain circumstances to make limited inquiries on marital status, age and public assistance, but you cannot be denied credit or receive credit on less favorable terms merely because of these factors. 15 U.S.C. 1691. California law also has some valuable protections. Civil Code Section 1812.30.

A. SEX AND MARITAL STATUS

California law specifically guarantees equality of treatment in receiving credit to women and unmarried people.

45

A woman, whether married or not, cannot be denied credit in her own name where a man having the same amount of earnings and other property would receive credit. Nor can she be offered credit on terms less favorable than a man in the same circumstances.

An unmarried person cannot be denied credit if a married person with the same amount of earnings and property would receive it. Neither can an unmarried person be offered credit on less favorable terms than those offered a married person in the same circumstances. Civ. Code Section 1812.30.

Moreover, women (or men) who receive spousal and child support payments under a written agreement or court order may include these amounts in their "earnings." The bank can, however, check to make sure the payments are "reliable," i.e., that they have been regularly made and paid in full.

Pensions, social security, disability or survivorship benefits and other similar sources of income are also considered earnings.

B. CREDIT BUREAU FILES IN YOUR OWN NAME

Credit bureaus must now file new credit information separately under the names of each person or spouse rather than under a joint account. A married or divorced woman can use her birth given name (or any other name) and not have to refer to her husband or former husband's name to gain access to her credit file. [Civ. Code Section 1812.30(e).]

If you are or were married and a credit bureau has you included in a joint credit file established before 1977, you can request either in writing or in person that the information be (as is done with information since January 1, 1977) filed separately under both names. [Civ. Code Section 1812.30(f).]

If you are thinking of ever obtaining credit, it is important that you request this change. This is because accounts of married people, even those opened in the names of both spouses, are often reported in only the husband's name. This has been generally true regardless of who has been paying the bills or whose income was used to obtain the account. Thus many married women do not have a credit history in their own names, though their husbands do.*

---

* You should definitely request that the change be made in the reporting of your credit history now. A divorced or widowed woman does not clearly have the same right to demand credit in the name of her former or deceased spouse as she does while she is still married.

C. IF ACTION IS TAKEN ON YOUR CREDIT
AND YOU'RE NOT SATISFIED

Federal and state law require that if: 1) you are denied credit; 2) you are refused credit in substantially the amount or the terms you requested; 3) there is a change in the terms of the credit arrangement you've had; or 4) your credit is revoked, you are entitled to a statement of reasons explaining why.

Some creditors provide this statement as a matter of course, most do not. You are entitled to request the statement within 60 days after you have been notified of the creditor's decision. The creditor must then respond within 30 days after receiving your request. In most instances, you are entitled to a written statement if you make a written request for it. Otherwise it may be oral (Civ. Code Section 1787.2 and 15 U.S.C. Section 1691).

D. IF YOU'RE DISSATISFIED WITH
THE TREATMENT YOU'VE RECEIVED

If you feel that a bank or other creditor has discriminated against you or has not followed the law, you have a number of places to turn to for help.

Begin by contacting the state Attorney General's office (see above). Also contact the Federal Trade Commission (F.T.C.). (See Chapter 2.)

Under state and federal law, you are entitled to your actual damages and punitive damages up to $10,000 plus attorneys' fees if you've been discriminated against. Contact an attorney. If you don't know any, see Chapter 3.

Unfortunately, although the law is clear on how banks and credit card companies can score a woman's credit, in reality it is somewhat different. Banks still often ignore these laws as evidenced by the more than 10,000 complaints relating to credit discrimination received by the F.T.C. in a recent year. Various women's rights organizations such as the Women's Credit Rights Project at the University of Southern California report that only a few cases have been brought to court and even then, proving discrimination is indeed difficult.

CHAPTER 5

UNDERSTANDING YOUR DEBTS

A. COMMON SENSE

There are as many ways of thinking about debts as there are people. However, before you can make any sensible headway you must know where you are starting from. What is your income? How much do you owe, to whom and for what?

CHART 1: Start by finding out exactly what you take in each month from all sources:

Jobs	_____
Social Security	_____
Pensions	_____
Public Assistance	_____
Disability	_____
Other	_____
Total	_____

CHART 2: Now list what it costs you to live each month (don't include any debt payments here except those necessary to that month such as a car or mortgage payment).

Monthly Expenses	
Food	———
Housing (rent, mortgage)	———.
Medical Expenses	———
Property Taxes	———
Utilities	———
Telephone	———
Transportation (car payment, repairs, public transit fees, gas)	———
Daily Expenses (lunch money, etc.)	———
Home Repair	———
Druggist	———
Dentist	———
Clothing	———
Church	———
Recreation	———
Other	———
Total	———

CHART 3: Now list all of your debts in their order of importance (you will want to read the rest of this chapter to understand the difference between secured and unsecured debts).*

	Mo. Payment	Amount Behind	Total Owed
Secured Debts			
Car (1)			
(2)			
Mortgage			
Finance Co. (1)			
(2)			
(3)			
Unsecured Debts			
Child Support			
Hospital Bills			
Doctor (1)			
(2)			
(3)			
Dentist			
Credit Cards (1)			
(2)			
(3)			

* Interest is collectable on debts if it was called for in the original agreement between creditor and debtor. Collection agencies can continue to add on interest at the rate called for in the original sales agreement. Once a court judgment is entered, interest can only be charged at 7%.

Club Dues
Dress Shop
Hardware Store
Department Store
Record Club
Attorney

You may now find it helpful to make a mark next to all of your debts. (X) for those that you consider it essential to pay such as rent, utilities, child support, car payment, etc. (Y) for those which are somewhat less important such as, perhaps, the dentist, doctor, and oil company, and (O) for those which aren't pressing at all such as the health club, airlines, and department store. Of course, one of the items in the non-essential category may suddenly become more important if a creditor gets a judgment against you and threatens to attach your wages (see Chapter 9 and 10).

NOTE—The money you have available to pay debts is that left over after you meet your essential monthly expenses (in Chart 2). If nothing is left over and you still have past due bills, you will want to think about the various strategies outlined in this book. Do not, under any circumstances, make payments on non-essential debts (such as the dress shop) when you haven't paid for essential services.

Now we ask you to learn a little law. Whether you have had any legal training or not it's important that you understand the difference between your secured and unsecured debts.

IMPORTANT—You may think that this sort of advice is obvious, but it doesn't seem to be. We have seen so many sensible people panic when pressured by bill collectors and make payments on non-essential items only to face eviction because they can't pay the rent, or have their lights turned off because they let the utility bill slide.

B. KNOW THE DIFFERENCE BETWEEN SECURED AND UNSECURED DEBTS

A debt is a debt is a debt, isn't that right? Well, not quite. There are two legal classifications of common debts and it's important that you understand the difference. It's not complicated and you can always flip back to this chapter if you have trouble keeping them straight.

1. Unsecured Debts
[most common debts]

If you borrow five dollars from a friend, you are in debt. If you don't pay the debt, your friend can sue you in Small Claims Court, get a judgment and try to collect it. He could go after your wages, your bank account or your property if he can find any not exempt under California law (see chapters 10, 11 and 12). Obviously this whole procedure is fairly cumbersome and time consuming. You would have plenty of opportunity to protect yourself while your friend would have to do quite a bit of work to get his money. Most debts operate this way and are called unsecured debts.

Unsecured debts include (this is not a complete list):
a) doctor bills
b) credit cards of all types
c) store revolving charge accounts*
d) loans with no collateral (whether from friends, banks, credit unions, etc.)
e) attorney fees
f) club dues
g) utility bills**
h) union dues**
i) rent**

IMPORTANT: On unsecured debts the creditor has no right to the return of any merchandise or property. Thus, if you bought a dress, didn't pay and then went bankrupt, you wouldn't have to return the dress.

---

*Be careful of this one. Most stores don't sell major items such as furniture and expensive applicances without getting a separate security agreement. See section B 2 of this chapter.

**While these debts are not secured, failure to pay them can result in immediate unpleasantness such as being evicted, having the lights turned off or losing your union membership.

2. Secured Debts

Now let's assume that your friend anticipated having trouble collecting the five dollars and required that you pledge your portable radio as security for the loan, and got you to agree in writing that if the loan was not repaid within two weeks he could take the radio. After two weeks he could sue you, get a judgment, and instead of going through the complicated steps necessary to collect the money, could simply repossess the radio to satisfy the debt.

Most debts in California are unsecured, but some specific types are usually secured. You have a secured debt when you have signed a contract (called a security agreement) which pledges some item of your property to be turned over to the creditor if you should fail to pay. Large expensive items are most likely to involve security agreements. If you buy large items such as furniture and major appliances, the seller will usually have you sign a security agreement. The same thing happens with new and used cars where the seller or lending institution keeps the pink slip until you make the last payment. A house mortgage involves exactly the same principle. If you fail to pay on any of these items, the creditor may quickly move to repossess or foreclose.*

In addition to the items mentioned above, you commonly have secured debts for boats, mobile homes, and snow mobiles. Many, but not all, loans from finance companies, banks, and credit unions are also secured. Security for these loans is often household furniture, or your car if you have finished paying for it.

3. Differences Between Collecting Secured And Unsecured Debts

As we pointed out with the example of the radio, it is much easier to collect on a secured than an unsecured debt. There are several reasons for this.

---

*Where furniture, appliances or other items of personal property are involved the creditor would more likely elect to attach your wages. See chapters 9 and 10.

1. In one situation (motor vehicles, see chapter 6), a secured item can simply be grabbed if you miss a payment. In other secured debt situations, the repossession of an item can follow directly from the judgment (see chapters 9 and 11). On unsecured debts there is absolutely no right to take possession of the goods at any time.

2. The California exemption laws which allow a family to keep their house, car, furniture, etc. (see chapter 11) don't protect you from a secured debt on the item itself. For example, if you bought a living room set on a sales contract that gave the seller the right to take the furniture if you didn't pay for it, you could not fail to pay and keep the furniture by claiming that it was exempt under the California law. Of course whether you finished paying for the living room set or not, you would be protected by the exemption laws from having it taken and sold to satisfy any other debt, secured or unsecured. As you now know, if you got the living room set in the first place without a security agreement you have no problem.

The same reasoning applies to all other secured debts. If you have a house, for example, filing a declaration of homestead (see chapter 12) protects your equity from almost all debts, but it will not protect you from the holder of the mortgage. Thus, if you pay your mortgage, your doctor or the credit card company cannot touch your homesteaded house. However, if you pay the doctor and the credit card company but neglect the mortgage, the homestead won't help you.

3. Even in bankruptcy there are differences between secured and unsecured debts. Bankruptcy will wipe out both, but with secured debts you must return the item in question* to discharge the debts while with ordinary unsecured debts you get to keep the goods and discharge the debt too. Don't get worried about this rule now, though. It's fully discussed in chapter 18 and you will find that there are ways to keep secured property such as your car and furniture for far less than the original debt.

4. Effect Of Returning Secured Item To Creditor

In many situations, the return of the secured item (couch, rug,

---

* Actually, you have three choices: (1) you can accept the creditor's estimate of value of the item, pay the amount, and keep the property; (2) decide to let the creditor repossess; or (3) disagree with the creditor's estimate of value but retain the property by making a deal.

T.V., etc.) ends the obligation.* Thus, if you owe $500 on a T.V. and can't pay, the debt is wiped out if the T.V. is returned. There is a catch, however: the merchant or collection agency must be willing to accept the property. Being business people they will usually do this only if they think that the item or property is worth more in a resale transaction than the debt. Often a used and possibly damaged piece of furniture will be worth very little on resale. Under normal circumstances, for example, a finance company would prefer to try and collect a debt on a T.V. for $500 rather than take the T.V. back if it would sell for only $200. Their attitude would be much different, however, if a person were judgment proof or contemplating bankruptcy.

IMPORTANT—It is crucial that you know the difference between secured and unsecured debts. If you don't understand now, reread this chapter. It will probably be helpful to make a list of all your debts and identify which category each is in. Remember, you can get a copy of your contract from the creditor if you are in doubt as to its terms. As a general rule it is better to pay secured debts before unsecured debts if you want to keep the secured item.

5. Debts and Divorce

The whole area of community and separate property and community and separate debts is discussed in detail in *The People's Guide to California Marriage and Divorce Law*, Warner & Ihara, Nolo Press, $7.95. Problems most commonly develop when a judge orders one spouse to pay certain debts and that person fails to do so. The creditor then proceeds against the other spouse, who normally feels very put upon, because under the divorce order the debts aren't his or her responsibility.

The law unfortunately is simple. Both spouses are still on the hook to the creditor no matter what the divorce decree says and the creditor can proceed against either. If the spouse who was **not** ordered to pay under the divorce decree ends up paying the creditor, that spouse does have a legal right to recover from the other spouse. Unfortunately, as we learn throughout this book, having a legal right and being able to enforce it aren't always the same thing.

---

*This rule does not apply to banks and finance companies, which advance money and take security in return. Also it does not apply to any motor vehicle (see chapter 6).

CHAPTER 6

REPOSSESSION BEFORE COURT ACTION—MOTOR VEHICLES

A. IT'S MOSTLY ILLEGAL

Until a few years ago your wages, bank account, and property could be taken from you **without** a court decision that your creditor was entitled to them. It's hardly believable but true, nevertheless. This sort of thing was legal because finance companies, collection agencies, banking associations, and retailers spent a lot of money on political campaigns and lobbyists to see that the legislature did nothing to threaten their profits. It has only been in the last six or seven years that a series of court decisions has resulted in an almost universal rule that it is unconstitutional to take wages or property from a person before he has his day in court. All these decisions have been won by underpaid, overworked legal aid lawyers! Now you know why many conservatives including collection agencies, finance companies and the like are out to kill legal aid. In the meantime, higher consumer awareness has resulted in there being lots of people who care whether or not loan sharks are writing the laws which affect your lives. More people caring about the rules has begun to result in better rules.

Today no one can take your wages or bank account without going to court and getting a judgment against you (see chapters 9 and 10) with the exception of the state and federal governments enforcing claims for unpaid taxes (see chapter 16). Similarly, no one can enter your home and take any item of your property without suing you, getting a judgment and then turning the judgment over to the sheriff or marshal (see chapters 8 and 9). The fact that you owe money on an item secured by a contract which says they can enter and take the item if you fall behind in payments makes no difference. This sort of contract provision is no longer enforceable. Of course, a creditor may try to talk you into voluntarily returning a piece of property. You may wish to do this because, as we have mentioned in chapter 5, in many situations your entire debt is cancelled when the secured item is returned, or you may want to avoid being sued and having court costs and attorney fees added to the judgment. There is, however, absolutely no requirement that you return any item voluntarily no matter how many payments you have missed. [If you are judgment proof (see chapter 1), you may want to keep the goods as long as possible, since the amount of the judgment may be of little importance to you.] Don't let anyone threaten you into doing anything you don't want to do. No one can send a truck to your home to get your furniture or send the police out because you have missed a payment. If you receive a threat, complain to the Collection Agency Licensing Bureau, 1430 Howe Ave., Sacramento, CA 95825, [916] 920-6424.

B. MOTOR VEHICLE REPOSSESSIONS

Motor vehicles (cars, trucks, and motorcycles, but not mobile* homes or boats) and motor vehicle financing is a huge business with huge profits. At every level of our society people in this business are used to getting their own way. Bill collecting is no

---

* Mobile homes — those which are stationary and need not be licensed under the Vehicle Code are exempt from the special strict deficiency judgment and prejudgment repossession rules discussed in this chapter. However, motor homes — those vehicles which must be licensed — are treated like cars, trucks and motorcycles and are subject to the repossession and deficiency judgment rules discussed here. (See Civil Code Section 1802.1.) Also see Chapter 11(b)(5), where we discuss exemptions from attachments for housetrailers and mobile homes you reside in.

exception. Most things that we have set forth about the rules that protect the consumer from unfair collection practices do not apply to motor vehicles. Motor vehicles can be repossessed without a law suit even having been filed. In fact, they can be repossessed if you miss a payment by one day. All the creditor has to do is go out and take the vehicle. You need not even be notified before they take it. As cutthroat as it sounds, it's also perfectly legal.

In practice it's unlikely that a vehicle would be picked up because a payment is a day or two late, but we have seen it happen where a finance company or bank learns some facts that convince them that a person's credit situation has gotten much worse. This might happen if a wife calls up the finance company to say that she has left her husband because he has lost his job and been arrested. Normally the legal owner (the person who has the pink slip) will call you or write a letter or two before they come after the vehicle. Still, if you are going to have to be a little late with your payment, it's a wise idea to call the lender to let them know what's happening. In most cases, especially if you have a decent past record and appear to be sincere, they will work with you rather than pick up the car. After all, the bank is in the money business, not the used car business. A little caution is always sensible however — don't tell them where the car is until you reach an understanding.

Finance companies are the most likely to grab a motor vehicle as soon as a payment is missed. Banks are a little less likely to move quickly and credit unions are fairly patient. When the decision is made to pick up a vehicle the debtor is not notified. The creditor hires a person who specializes in legally "stealing" cars, and supplies the debtor's address, place of business, etc. The repossessor then hunts the vehicle. Often he will find it sitting in front of the debtor's house or in the driveway. He will then wait until the debtor is asleep, call the police to tell them what he is doing and then, using a master key, if possible, or hot wiring if not, simply drive off. If the vehicle is in a locked garage the repossessor can not legally break in to get it as this would leave him open to be sued. Some repossessors will take a vehicle from an unlocked garage when they only have to open the door, and some will not. They will all grab a vehicle in the driveway or under a car port. If the vehicle is not near the house, a search will be made in the neighborhood. Most people who think that their car, truck, or motorcycle may be repossessed will make some effort to hide it. They won't go to too much trouble, however, as that would cancel out the convenience of having the vehicle in the first place. Many times people park a car about three blocks from their home when they fear repossession, far enough away to be hard to find, but close enough to still be convenient. The repossessors have long since learned this little bit of psychology, however, and often find the vehicle within minutes after the start of the search. Leaving the motor vehicle in the locked garage of a neighbor is probably the best way to protect it.*

IMPORTANT—No one has the right to take a motor vehicle from your personal possession without your consent. If anyone tries to take the vehicle while you are present, they are legally liable for any harm done you or the property that is reasonably related to their actions. You have the right to protect yourself and the motor vehicle without liability to yourself, but you can not start any hostile or violent behavior if none is used against you.

C. GETTING YOUR MOTOR VEHICLE BACK

After a vehicle is repossessed the creditor will sell it. Ten days written **notice of intent to sell** must be given all persons who signed the purchase contract (this includes co-signers). This notice must be handed to the debtor personally, or sent by certified mail, return receipt requested, to the debtor's address as shown on the contract unless the debtor has notified the creditor of a

---

* A dealer might argue that you were concealing the car in order to avoid repossession. If the judge goes along with his position, you would lose the right to reinstate the contract. Civil Code Section 2983.2. (See Section C, below.)

change of address. The notice must give the debtor a full accounting of all money paid and owed and give him/her 15 days (20 if s/he resides outside of California) to "redeem" the car. This means that if the debtor pays the full amount of the contract balance within 15 days s/he can get the car back. If the debtor requests, the seller must extend the redemption period for an additional 10 days.

If the car has been repossessed, California law provides the debtor the right to reinstate the contract of the automobile, but it also allows three broad exceptions to this right. The seller does not have to reinstate the contract if s/he "in good faith" determines that (1) the buyer provided false or misleading information on his or her credit application; (2) the buyer concealed or removed the car from the state to avoid repossession; or (3) the buyer has failed to take care of the car and it has, or may, become substantially reduced in value. (Civil Code Section 2983.3.) Although you can argue that the misinformation on your credit application was the result of an honest error and not of material importance anyway, or that you were parked in your neighbor's garage because it is cleaner, larger, more convenient, etc.; or that you did in fact take reasonable care of your car, it is pretty clear that these exceptions are so broad that they don't offer much protection. Nevertheless, the law does state that the seller must bear the burden of proof in justifying his refusal to reinstate the contract.

The buyer can only exercise his/her right of contract reinstatement once in any 12-month period and twice during the term of the contract. The buyer must make all payments in arrears, as well as any applicable delinquency charges. The buyer is also required to reimburse the seller for all reasonable and necessary collection and repossession costs and fees, including attorneys' fees and expenses related to the retaking and holding of the car.

1. Personal Property In Repossessed Motor Vehicles

You are entitled to the return of all personal property (i.e., books, clothes, tools, sporting equipment, etc.) left in a car that is repossessed. You are not entitled to the return of anything related to the car such as a spare tire or car radio. Simply contact the creditor and ask that your property be returned. They will normally be cooperative. If they are not, see a lawyer or consider bringing a suit in Small Claims Court.

D. AUTOMOBILE DEFICIENCY JUDGMENTS

You probably won't believe this one, so brace yourself. After the motor vehicle is repossessed, the creditor can turn around and sell it wholesale at a car auction or to a used car lot for far less than its retail value and sue you for the difference between what you still owe on the contract and what he sold the vehicle for. For example: You agreed to pay $4,000 for a car, paid $800 down and then another $1,200 in payments before you lost your job and missed several payments. The balance owed on the contract is $2,000. The car can then be repossessed and sold wholesale. Assuming the car could be sold retail for $2,000 with a newspaper ad, it might bring $1,200 wholesale to a used car lot, perhaps less, as wholesale auto sales in this situation are notoriously dishonest. You would then be sued and would find yourself with a "deficiency" judgment against you for $800 (the difference between the $2,000 you owed at the time of repossession and the $1,200 that the creditor sold the car for), plus repossession costs, sales costs and legal fees. It stinks, doesn't it. Well it doesn't smell much better when the money is being passed around the state capitol to keep the law on the books. Every consumer organization in the state has supported legislation to do away with motor vehicle "deficiency" judgments, with no success. It has been getting closer in recent years, but the auto lobby still seems to have more bucks than consumers have votes. Little people are still paying thousands in car payments, losing their cars, and getting nailed with huge judgments. And they say we live in the land of the free.

Legislation to do away with "deficiency" judgments is again before the legislature. You can help by writing your State Senator or Assemblyman.

REMINDER—Repossessions without a court judgment, and "deficiency" judgments apply only to motor vehicles and not to other types of personal property.* Furniture, for example, can be repossessed only after judgment and there can be no law suit for the difference between what you owe and the amount the property is sold for. And with anything but motor vehicles, if the creditor takes the property back at any time, that's the end of the debtor's obligation.

---

* There are no deficiency judgments on motor homes. Civil Code Section 2983.8.

517 Kindy Drive
Bakersfield, California
July 1, 19___

State Senator_____
State Capitol
Sacramento, California 95814

Dear Senator_____,

　　The present laws on automobile repossessions without getting a judgment are very unfair. The parts that allow deficiency judgments are also bad. Please support legislation to outlaw both of these practices.

　　It's time the little guy got a break.

Very truly yours,

Marcia Kemp

E. MOTOR VEHICLE REPAIR LAWS

A person who repairs a car or motorcycle (mobile homes which don't need to be registered are not included) is entitled to be paid for labor and materials when the car is picked up, as long as the repairs are made for a dollar amount authorized by the vehicle owner. If a written statement of charges for completed work is presented to the owner and the owner does not pay, California law entitles the repairperson to initiate proceedings to sell the vehicle if within 30 days he or she either applies for an authorization to conduct a lien sale or files an action in court.

　　If the vehicle has a value over $300, and the bill is not paid within 30 days (15 days if the vehicle is worth between $100 and $300), the repairperson must send to the legal owner (bank or finance company) and the registered owner, by certified mail, a written notice of intent to sell and a blank Declaration of Opposition form. S/he must also state that the owner has a right to a hearing in court. If the owner sends back the Declaration of Opposition form to the Department of Motor Vehicles within 15 days requesting a court hearing, then the repairperson can sell the vehicle only if s/he obtains a court judgment or release from the owner. (See Cal. Civil Code Sections 3071 and 3072 for more details.)

If the vehicle is sold, the proceeds of the sale are applied to pay off the repair bill, storage costs and actual selling costs (not to exceed $50). The balance is forwarded to the Department of Motor Vehicles and the legal owner then files a claim requesting the balance. The D.M.V. does not have to honor claims which are filed more than three years after the sale.

At any time before the sale the owner may get his/her vehicle back by paying the repair bill plus the storage costs and the actual costs incurred in sale preparations (not to exceed $50). After the sale, the legal owner may redeem a car worth more than $300 by paying the amount of sale, plus all costs and interests of the sale, together with 12% interest. This must be done within 10 days after the sale and does not apply to vehicles worth less than $300. [See Cal. Civil Code 3071(i).]

In any event, any portion of a bill for repair work or services which is in excess of $500 or storage in excess of $400 is invalid unless the repairperson has given actual notice in writing to the legal owner and has obtained his/her consent *before* beginning the repairs.

IMPORTANT—If you get into a dispute with a repairman over motor vehicle repairs, it is wise to get your car back first and argue later. We know of people who, after concluding that they were being cheated, paid the garage by check and then stopped payment on the check after they got the car back. Of course this sort of approach is liable to result in the garageman starting a law suit against you. A more moderate course would be to complain to the State of California Bureau of Automobile Repair, which is listed in all metropolitan phone books. Still another possibility, if the bill is over $50, is to pay it with a credit card and then argue about it later with the credit card company. This procedure is discussed in detail in Chapter 14D.

CHAPTER 7

HOW TO DEAL WITH BILL COLLECTORS*

Bill collecting is big business, and just like any other big business the idea is to make as much money as possible. This means that lots of people like you are going to have to cough up lots of cash. How you should respond to bill collectors depends upon what you want from them. You may want extra time to pay. Or to lower the size of your payments. Or not to pay at all. Whatever your objective, always keep this in mind: **Bill collectors work on the psychology of fear.** If they have you scared, they have you. As you will find out by reading this chapter, there is really not much they can do to you. If you're afraid, you'll do a lot worse to yourself than they can ever do. So decide on your best course of action and be firm about it. If you stick to your guns and don't panic, you will be able to take those sensible steps necessary to take care of your debts and sleep well in the process.

---

* We are often asked if, once a bill is turned over to a collection agency, interest is still collectable. The answer is yes. If interest was called for on the original debt, the collection agency can keep adding it on at the same rate until a court judgment is entered at which time the interest rate becomes 7% (see Chapter 8).

A. WHEN BILLS START TO PILE UP

One day the mail arrives and there are several letters from companies with whom you have accounts suggesting politely that perhaps you have overlooked their last bill. If it's convenient they would appreciate your paying it. This, of course, is a form letter that goes out automatically on every account that is overdue. If you fail to respond to the first letter there will be more. Most companies send out their notices by computer. The computer, in effect, holds a package of these notices and merely sends one out after another, waiting a certain period of time between mailings. Each notice is a little stiffer and more threatening than the last, until finally you will be told that if you don't pay immediately, your account will be turned over to an attorney for legal action. This is nonsense. The creditor will give the account to a collection agency which will take **at least** several months to start a law suit.

The content of the letters varies from company to company. Some remind you of how valuable your credit rating is, while others spend more time trying to convince you of the wretchedness of law suits, wage attachments, and repossessions. Some companies will phone you one or more times to ask you when they can expect a payment, some will not.

Most large companies such as department stores, gasoline retailers, clothing stores, etc., have small collection departments. These are the people who send the first few letters. Normally they do not get heavy, and rarely resort to harassment because they believe it's bad for their public image to be identified as hard hearted scrooge types. There are also favorable tax laws which allow the company to deduct the value of the merchandise from their income, resulting in very little out of pocket loss. After several form letters and a phone call or two fail to get you to pay, they will turn the account over to an independent collection agency. Of course, a month or two after your first payment is overdue, they will cancel your credit privileges.

1. Need More Time To Pay?

Often when the first notices of overdue accounts arrive you will want to pay the bills, but will be temporarily short of funds. All you need is a little extension of time from your creditors. Your best bet is to ask for it directly and politely. Write a letter on all of your overdue accounts and explain what the problem is and when they may expect you to catch up on your payments. If you can send a part payment this will be helpful, but it is not absolutely necessary. Even a token payment of $5 or $10 tends to be some indication of good faith. You might write something along the lines of the letter on the next page.

CAUTION: This approach works a lot better with the original creditor than it does with a collection agency. Professional bill collectors often view reasonableness as weakness (see B, below).

If this fails to pacify the creditor, or if you believe that circumstances require a little more clout, you might consider visiting a lawyer and having him write the letter to your creditors (see chapter 3). The lawyer will not say anything much different than you would, but his stationery alone will guarantee that more respect is given the letter. The creditor knows, too, that if he doesn't cooperate with the lawyer's request for more time, the lawyer is likely to recommend bankruptcy.

IMPORTANT—In reading letters or taking phone calls from creditors, do not allow yourself to be scared or intimidated into any unwise actions. After reading this book you should have a clear idea of your situation and how to handle it. Don't alter your plan without good reason. If you have decided that your first priority is your home payment, your second priority is buying food and your third is your car payment, don't allow the dress shop to talk you into sending them $50 unless the important items have been taken care of.

REMINDER—Anxiety! This is your worst enemy and your creditor's main weapon. **Relax,** enjoy your supper and keep the bills in perspective. Some of the wisest, finest people in history were late on their bills. Who really cares that Mark Twain was always in debt. We remember him for his beautiful words, not for his fiscal problems with the butcher. Only you can make yourself

45 Ayse Street
San Leandro, California
May 12, 19___

Honorable Al's Toggery
100 Broadway
Oakland, California

Dear Sirs:

I just received your notice that I am overdue in paying my account. I am very concerned about this and have failed to pay only because several family emergencies have prevented me from doing so. These include [*being laid off, sick, disabled, unexpected tax obligation, illness to family member or whatever other excuse you have or can think up*].*

My financial situation will improve in the near future. [*Mention any particularly promising facts such as returning to work, getting a raise, getting a workmen's compensation award, selling property, etc.*] I expect to be able to pay you on August 15, 19___.

I will appreciate any consideration you can give me. Should you wish to discuss this matter, please feel free to call me at 765-4321 in the evening.**

Very truly yours,

Zeynep Kora

*One common reason for failure to pay bills is divorce or separation. In this situation there is rarely enough money to maintain two households. Creditors know this and get very nervous when they hear of a divorce or separation, so as a general rule it's better not to list this reason.

**Don't put down a work phone number unless the creditor already knows where you work.

anxious and miserable. Your creditors will do everything in their power to encourage you to do it, but they have no real power. Remember, it feels good to smile.

B. COLLECTION AGENCIES—HOW THEY OPERATE

This is the guts of the bill collection process. Sooner or later most unpaid bills, whatever the source, are turned over to collection agencies.* If you take a little time to understand how these agencies work, you will be way ahead when you deal with them. Some of the information contained in this section also applies to company bill collections, but is put here because it is most often used by collection agencies.

Most people in most collection agencies are paid to be nasty, brutal, and to hang on to you like a blood-thirsty tick. Occasionally you find someone with a little human understanding in this business, but don't count on it. Most collectors work on the theory that if you are harassed often enough, you will get some money up somehow. There are tens of thousands of collection agencies in this country and many of them are very prosperous so you can see that these tactics work.

Collection agencies are private business operations which specialize in collecting overdue accounts. They usually take the accounts from the original creditor (store, doctor, credit union, etc.) with the understanding that they receive a percentage of any money recovered, with the rest going back to the creditor. The percentage the collection agency gets varies, usually depending on how easy the debt is to collect. A collection agency will have a relatively easy time collecting overdue accounts forwarded by reputable stores and well managed credit unions where careful credit checks are made before credit is extended. The debtor will probably be fairly easy to locate, capable of working and not particularly hostile to the original creditor. One-third of the amount recovered would be a typical collection agency fee for this type of account. However, a collection agency trying to collect the accounts of a credit jeweler with a

---

* On occasion, businesses will fake turning accounts over to collection agencies. They simply buy forms with a phony collection agency name on top and send them out themselves. If you get a letter from a collection agency, look in the phone book to see if they really exist. A variation of this scheme is a collection agency which offers creditors a series of dun letters, with little or no other collection activity except listing the debtor as a bad credit risk. The theory of this sort of collection effort—which is particularly likely to be used for small bills such as magazine subscriptions, doctor bills, etc.—is that lots of people will pay if they receive a series of dun letters, but if they don't pay, it's simply too expensive to sue.

dubious reputation for honesty, a health spa, or a cut rate meat outfit would certainly demand a higher percentage, probably at least fifty percent of the original debt and perhaps more. Sometimes a collection agency will simply purchase old debts from the creditor and try to collect more than the price they paid for the debt. This is unusual. The percentage method is the one normally used.

Collection agencies have their own bureaucracy. They operate on a volume basis. At any one time they have thousands of accounts (some of the big ones have tens of thousands). On most of these they will recover little or nothing, often because they simply can't locate the debtors. Collectors operate by trying to identify those accounts where success looks likely from those where it does not, and then going after the former full speed ahead.

When you receive a dun letter after the original debtor has given up, you can be sure that it's from a professional collector. Don't be misled by such names as Central Adjustment Service, Associated Credit Bureau, or Bureau of Medical Economics. You are only dealing with a collection agency. Don't take letters on legal stationery too seriously. Collection agencies have close working relationships with attorneys and commonly send out hundreds of form letters over the attorney's rubber stamped signatures, hoping to scare you. The attorney usually never sees the actual letters; they are sent directly from the collection agency's office. In many cases no lawsuit is actually filed. It's cheap to threaten, expensive to sue. Some collection agencies never file lawsuits, especially for small bills (i.e., anything under $200–$300).*

1. They Can't Hurt You If They Can't Find You

There are lots of reasons why you may have no desire to negotiate a settlement. Perhaps you have so many debts that only bankruptcy makes sense (see chapter 18), or you may be judgment proof (see chapter 1), or you may simply not want to pay for any number of other reasons.

Whatever your situation, remember a collection agency or other creditor can't sue you, take your wages, harass you by mail or phone or otherwise bother you if they can't locate you.

---

* It is a violation of the Fair Debt Collection Practices Law for a creditor to falsely threaten to sue. He can be liable for your actual damages and for a penalty of $100–$1000.

People move a lot these days and often change jobs. Many times a debtor can't be located by the time an account has been turned over for collection. Moving a long distance is a particularly good way to avoid a creditor. This is because collection agencies are local and are simply not organized to collect debts out of state.*There is a procedure by which a collection agency in one part of the country can assign a debt or judgment to a collection agency located at the place where you have moved, but forwarded debts do not receive the same time and attention as do local ones. The commission in these cases must be split between two collection agencies making this type of collection far less profitable. In addition, a collection agency half way across the country from the original creditor can expect little if any repeat business and has no incentive to put much effort into a difficult collection.

NOTE—When dealing with a collection agency located far from the creditor, you can gain a breathing space by raising several questions about the debt. For example, you might question the accuracy of the balance claimed to be owed, or state that you never received one of the items in question. Before proceeding, the agency will have to check out the questions with the forwarding collection agency which in turn will have to check with the original creditor. This often slows things down several months.

When a collection agency gets an account, they also get all the information that the original creditor has about you. This will include your address, phone, place of work, bank, car registration number and whatever else appeared on the original credit application. The collection agency will first try to write or call you. Often they use the certified letter, registered letter, or telegram ploy. They hope you will sign for one of these, thereby telling the agency where you are.

If you have moved, the agency will check the post office for a forwarding address and of course will examine the phone books for the greater metropolitan area. Should this fail, the next step is to call your job with the collector posing as a friend or business associate. If you have changed jobs, the collector

---

* There are several "national" collection agencies - Equifax, TRW, etc. - but even they are no where near as efficient at tracking debtors around the country as they would like to have you believe.

will often pretend to be a long lost friend or relative and try to worm your new location out of an unsuspecting friend. They have a lot of experience at this and are often totally convincing. Another common strategy is to try and get the personnel department to give them the address to which they sent your W-2 tax forms. Again the collector poses as a friend of yours.

If the above fails, the next step is to contact the Department of Motor Vehicles to see if you have informed them of your new address. Collectors can get this information for $2.00 and are presently, through the state association of collection agencies, fighting all proposed legislation aimed at making D.M.V. information confidential.* Another tactic often used is to check with the Registrar of Voters in the county of your last residence. If you have reregistered in the county, the registrar will have your new address. Also the collector is likely to check the criss-cross, or street address phone directory published by the phone company. This will tell him the names and phone numbers of your near neighbors. By calling neighbors and posing as a friend it's often possible to find out where you have moved especially if you haven't warned the neighbors. Unlisted numbers and numbers where no address is listed don't appear in the criss-cross directory. Also utilities such as the electric company may have a new address if you have moved within their service area, but several collectors indicate that this information is hard to get. Most collection agencies will not do a great deal more beyond listing the debtor's name with the local credit bureau on the locate list.** In some cases they may try to contact friends or relations listed on the original credit application, but they won't push to search too hard.*** It is not profitable for them to do so. They make their money from the large number of cases where they can find people fairly easily, not by extended man hunts for missing persons.

---

* The D.M.V. now requires the person making the request to have a legitimate reason for requesting the information (e.g., hit-and-run accident, debt, unpaid judgment, etc.). The person must identify him/herself and verify the identification. As soon as the person receives the information, you must be notified as to what information was provided and to whom it was provided. A record of all this is kept at the D.M.V. (Civil Code Section 1798.26.)

** This means that if you apply for credit in the same geographical area the collection agency will promptly be told of your whereabouts (see chapter 4).

*** One other technique is to check with the County Assessor's Office to find out who owns the house you moved out of — the collector then calls the landlord and tries to get your forwarding address.

NOTE—Creditors can't legally get your location from Social Security, Veterans, State Unemployment, Disability or Welfare Department records. This information is supposed to be confidential. There have been a few cases where government employees with access to the computerized records have been paid off. A collector friend tells us that the risk is too high in trying to get information from these sources and that he believes it is almost never done.

2. Negotiating A Settlement

By this point you should have a good grasp of your situation including the difference between your secured and unsecured debts (see chapter 5). If you are working or have some valuable property (such as land) that a creditor could grab, you should be particularly concerned to take defensive action before the collection agency draws blood. Remember, if you have not yet been sued (see chapter 8) and your auto (see chapter 6) and your home (see chapter 12) are protected, you have some breathing space. Your wages, bank account, and other property can't be taken until after a judgment has been entered in court except for tax obligations (see chapter 16). This can't occur until after you have been sued and have been served with legal papers (see chapter 8).

Collection agencies commonly accept cash settlements far below the full amount of the debt to avoid spending months trying to collect the whole thing. There is no rule as to how much they will accept to give you a complete release. We recommend an original offer of about one-third of the original debt amount for bargaining purposes. This is probably a little low, although we have seen a number of debts settled at this level where the agency believes that collection would be difficult or impossible in any other way. Settlement for forty to sixty percent of the debt is more normal, but it's always wise to start a little low. Full cash payment of the compromise amount (or at least a large initial payment) is almost always a condition to this sort of arrangement. A collection agency clearly has a strong motive for accepting $250 on a $500 debt if they get the money in cash. They close their books, take their percentage and forget about you. There is little reason, however, for the agency to reduce the debt total if you offer payments. They still have to keep track of you and always face the possibility that after a payment or two you will again stop paying.

In negotiating, paint a bleak picture of your financial circumstances. Be sure to go into detail about illnesses, depressions, problems with work, etc. Make up a few problems if your story doesn't sound desperate enough. Of course, mentioning that you are seriously considering bankruptcy is always a good idea. Never tell a collection agency where you live, work, bank, or can be reached if they don't already know. Never send in a payment by a check from your bank. Use money orders and buy them at a place other than where you bank. If a collector asks for personal information, tell him simply and politely that the information is none of his business.

IMPORTANT—It is wise to contact a collection agency if, and only if, you decide to seriously negotiate. If you can't lay your hands on enough cash to make a realistic offer, don't call them. Your contact may be the very thing that lets the agency know your location. They send out thousands of form letters a month. A large number of these never connect with the debtor, so the fact that you have received a letter doesn't mean that they know where you are.

You might want to think about having a lawyer help you with your negotiating. Following the same reasoning mentioned in section A of this chapter, the attorney, just by being an attorney, commands more respect than you do. Of course this is a silly way to run the world, but it's still true. Also, an attorney has negotiated hundreds of similar cases and should have a pretty good intuition as to the best settlement possible in your situation. Again, remember, mention of bankruptcy by an attorney carries considerably more clout than does your mention of it. Sure, it will cost you a few dollars to have the attorney make some phone calls and write some letters, but it shouldn't cost a lot, and a decent attorney should more than earn his fee (see chapter 3). A nice side benefit of involving a lawyer is the California law prohibiting a collection agency from contacting you directly once they know you have an attorney. If they do, complain to the State at once. But, if you get a lawyer, be sure you know in advance what the lawyer will do and exactly what it will cost.

a. Negotiating A Settlement—Secured Debts

The fact that a debt is secured by an agreement stating that if the debt is not paid some item must be returned (such as furniture) doesn't change the basic strategy discussed above, but it does add another bargaining chip to the game. For discussion, let's assume you borrowed $1,500 from your credit union and pledged your living room set as security. A divorce has left you no money and a pile of debts, and this particular debt has been assigned to Blackbeard Bloodhound's Collection Agency. The furniture is pretty well worn, a few pieces have been junked, and you and your former wife have divided the rest which taken together are worth about $350.

When the people at Blackbeard Bloodhound's contact you, they are sure to threaten to take the furniture. As you know, they can't do this unless you give it to them voluntarily or they go to court and get a judgment. As a matter of strategy, however, you are probably best off inviting them to come and pick the furniture up. Unless they think you will never work again, they will not do this. The $1,000 debt is much more valuable than $350 worth of junky furniture. Remember, we learned in chapter 5 that if they take the furniture the $1,000 debt is completely cancelled. Therefore, where the secured item has little cash value, your negotiations are going to be almost the same as if it did not exist.

Now let's assume that the furniture pledged as security is quite valuable and includes a color T.V., a stereo in good condition, and has a resale value of close to $1,000. Now the collection agency would be more willing to take the security. Oh, they would still prefer money, because this saves them the trouble of picking up and selling the furniture, but their bargaining position is far stronger and they have little motive to settle the claim much below the $1,000 total.

3. Collection Agency Harassment—Legal And Illegal *

Collection agencies make a living by harassing people. Often there is a fine line separating harassing conduct that is legal from that which is illegal. If you can catch a collection agency on the wrong side of this line, you can often get the debt in question wiped out, by being smart and aggressive.

A collection agency can contact you by mail demanding payment, they can phone you. **But you can stop a collection agency from communicating with you entirely by simply telling them so in writing** (see sample letter, following). After this, they can no longer contact you except to tell you that they are taking some specific action, such as filing papers in court, or garnishing your wages.

A debt collector cannot legally do any of the following:

a) Use obscene or profane language;

b) Threaten to harm you or any family member or friend;

c) Threaten to publish, or actually publish your name publically as a person who does not pay bills;

d) Claim to be law enforcement officers of any kind or in any way suggest that they are conected with any federal, state, county or local government;**

e) Send you any written document that looks like a court form or government document;

f) Repeatedly use the telephone to annoy you;

g) Contact your employer, except to verify employment or for some act (i.e., a wage garnishment) necessary to actually collect the debt;

---

* No collection agency can legally contact you about a bill that you tell them you don't owe until they send you proof of the debt such as a copy of an unpaid bill. If you are confused about whether you owe money or not, you are entitled to ask for, and receive, a full statement as to the details of the alleged debt.

** Anyone that makes this sort of claim on any debt except a debt for child support is almost surely lying. Ask for names, badge numbers, supervisor's names, etc., and check it out.

h) Threaten to get welfare or unemployment benefits cut off (this of course can't be done).

i) Call you at work if you or your employer tell them not to. If this becomes a problem, put your request in writing and keep a copy;

j) Falsely pretend that you have committed a crime;

k) Falsely pretend that a legal action is being started against you when this is not true;

l) Threaten to take your property (i.e., your wages) unless they have a court judgment (see Chapters 8, 9).

m) Claim to be an attorney or use attorney's stationery when they are not;

n) Falsely claim that the debt will be increased by the addition of attorney's fees, service fees, finance charges, etc.

That collection agencies are not supposed to do any of the above doesn't mean they don't. In fact, abusive practices are still all too common. The authors of this book have seen all the above list used against low income people when they served as legal aid lawyers. It has been particularly common to send people fake legal papers or to call them and pretend to be a law enforcement officer. People are told, for example, that if they don't make a payment immediately, the sheriff will come and take all their furniture away or will have their wages immediately attached. That sort of thing is not still done, you say? Well, several southern California collectors have been caught pretending to be peace officers and have had their licenses suspended. Vulgarity and profanity are also common as are veiled threats against the debtor or members of his family. For example, if a collector knows that a debtor's son works for the highway patrol, he might threaten to tell the patrol that his parents are deadbeats. Tactics like this are completely illegal.

Fortunately, the State of California and the federal government have finally started to assume some responsibility to regulate the worst abuses of collection agencies. After years of doing nothing they have begun to clean things up a little. If you believe you have been treated unfairly by a collector, contact:*

State of California
Collection Agency Licensing
  Bureau
1430 Howe Avenue
Sacramento, California 95814

State of California Office
of the Attorney General
Consumer Fraud Division
555 Capitol Mall
Sacramento, California 95814

---

* The state and federal rules are very similar, but the California rules apply to all debt collectors (collection agencies and the original creditor) while the feds only regulate collection agencies. It's always best to complain to both agencies, if you have a problem.

and either

Federal Trade Commission   Federal Trade Commission
11000 Wilshire Blvd.   or   450 Golden Gate Ave.
Los Angeles,   Box 36005
   California 90024   San Francisco, California 94102

After you make your complaint, you will be supplied a complaint form and will be given help in dealing with the obnoxious collector. If the state agencies drag their feet, contact the local office of your State Senator or Assemblyman and tell them your problem. They will make sure that a thorough investigation of your complaint is made. Remember, keep all documents that shed light on your complaint and try, if possible, to have a friend listen in on any abusive oral conversations with the collection agency.

Collectors are used to bullying people. They don't know what to do when you take the offensive. Any time you have a well documented case of harassment, turn the tables on them. After complaining to the state and the F.T.C., try to get an attorney to represent you in a damage suit against the collection agency in either state or federal court (attorney fees and court costs can be recovered if you win. You are entitled to any actual damages (including pain and suffering) that you experience and up to $1000 in punitive damages ($2,500 if the violation was that they sent you a written document that appeared to be a court form, government document, or attorney's letter but it was not). Perhaps a more satisfying alternative would be to bring your own case to Small Claims Court. At the very least, write the original creditor and tell them what happened, sending a copy of the letter to the collection agency, the State Bureau of Collection and Investigative Services, your local State Senator and Assemblyman, and the Federal Trade Commission. If you persist and make enough of an issue out of it, you are likely to get the whole debt cancelled in exchange for shutting up. We have seen this approach work many times, as the original creditor may well be as disturbed by the collection agency's tactics as you are. A sample letter follows.

Bluebeard's Collection Agency
49 Pirate St.
Hooksville, California

Dear Sirs:

   I have received numerous phone calls and several letters from you concerning several debts that I haven't paid. As I have repeatedly informed you, I am not able to pay these bills.

   Accordingly under 15 USC 1692C this is my formal notice to you to CEASE ALL FURTHER COMMUNICATION with me except for the reasons specifically set forth in the federal law.

                                          Very truly yours,

                                          Lynn Smith

---

                                          15 Main Street
                                          Los Angeles, California
                                          July 12, 19___

Trueshine Furniture Factory
11 Maple Street
Cedarville, California

Dear Sirs:

   On May 10, 19___ I purchased a living room set from your company for $1,000 ($500 down and the rest at $50 per month). Soon after the purchase I lost my job and later became ill. I have had no money since to pay you. In 19___, I was contacted by the Bluebeard Bloodhound Collection Agency. They called me often, used profanity to me, my husband, and my eleven year old son. In addition, they sent a man to my house who claimed to be a county employee to get the furniture and on several occasions have called my father and threatened him with a law suit even though he is a 76 year old diabetic with a heart condition and has had no connection with this transaction.

   I have contacted the State of California Bureau of Collections and Investigative Services and they are conducting an investigation. In the meantime I am considering seeing an attorney. Frankly, I am at my wits end with these people and am fully prepared to take any steps necessary to protect myself and my family from further harassment. I am writing you in the hope that you have not condoned Bluebeard Bloodhound's practices and can do something to help me.

                                          Very truly yours,

                                          Lynn Smith

copies sent to:

_____ , State Assemblyman
California Bureau of Collection and Investigative Services
Bluebeard Bloodhound Collections
Federal Trade Commission

4. Turning The Tables On The Collection Agency

Unfortunately, there is still a good deal a collection agency can do to be unpleasant without engaging in illegal activity. Phone calls and dun letters are bad enough. But remember, the collection agency is trying to get you upset. Just relax, don't let the letters get to you, and hang up the phone as soon as you realize who is calling.

Here is an example of an actual conversation a friend of ours had with a bill collector. (We will call our friend "S"; "BC" stands for Bill Collector.)

BC: Hello, Mr. "S," I am calling about your charge account. It's overdue.

S: Yes, I know.

BC: Well, when can we expect a payment?

S: Not for another month or two.

BC: I'm sorry but we cannot accept that.

S: Well, there's nothing else I can do. We just don't have any money right now and won't have any next month.

BC: What is the problem, Mr. "S"?

S: It's personal and I would rather not talk about it.

BC: You realize that your credit rating will fall because of this.

S: Yes, I know, but I have no interest in buying more things on credit.

BC: And that it will hinder you from getting credit at other places.

S: Yes, but I just don't have any money right now and I am tired of paying high interest anyway.

BC: We can also attach your wages.

S: Yes, but not until you get a judgment and that takes time.

BC: Why, we have a battery of lawyers and can send them to court in fifteen minutes.

S: Yes, but you still must first serve me with papers, have a trial, and get a judgment before you can attach. This takes 30 days from the time you serve me with the papers which you have not done yet.

BC: You think you're so smart. Why, we can call your employer.

S: Yes, but you can only do it once.

BC: How did you know that? Oh (mumble, mumble), but once is enough anyway.

S: And besides you don't know who my employer is.

BC: Oh, we have ways of finding out.

S: And besides he wouldn't care.

Click—The bill collector hung up.

The bill collector tried to frighten the debtor with talk about his credit rating, attachment of his wages and calling his employer. But none worked. And so, having gone through his scare list with no results, the bill collector freaked out and, not knowing what else to say, hung up the phone.

A little laughter will often flip them out completely. We know of one person who simply called the collection agency three times for every time they called her and wasted as much of the agency's time as possible. She also would write poems about how uptight collection agencies are on the bottom of all the letters they sent and sent them back to the agency in an envelope with no stamp. Pretty soon every time she called, the collection agency would slam down the phone. Use your head, you're not helpless and you are only a victim if you let yourself be.

CHAPTER 8

THE LAW SUIT

If you fail to pay debts you will probably be sued sooner or later. This is because the creditor, with the exception of the tax man, can't go after your wages, bank account or property until he has sued you and gotten judgment. The period during which you can be sued ("statute of limitations") varies greatly for different sorts of debts. On written contracts (this covers almost everything you buy on credit) a law suit must be filed within four years or it is barred.* The statute of limitation period on oral contracts (i.e., an oral rental contract) is two years, on most personal injury claims such as auto accidents is one year, and for property damage is three years.** To figure when the statute of limitations runs out, start counting from the day that the loan was due. If payments are involved this means from the date you missed the payment.*** But be careful, you can voluntarily extend (revive) the statute of limitations if you agree to pay the debt in writing after the limitations period has run out.*** We are often asked if simply making a payment after statute of limitations period has expired without entering into a new written agreement will reinstate the debt? The answer is 'No'.

* Code of Civil Procedure Section 337.
** See C.C.P. Sections 338, 339, 339.5, 340.
*** C.C.P. Section 360.

Example 1: A buys furniture from B on a written installment contract. A pays B for one year and then ceases making payments. A has the right to sue B for four years from the date of the missed payment. After that the suit is barred by the statute of limitations.

Example 2: Same example but after A hasn't paid B for five years, B writes A a note and asks for a small payment as a token of good faith. A sends $10 - can B now sue A? No, simply making a payment doesn't revive the right to sue, but if A sent a note back to B with the money saying that he would pay so much each month, the suit would be revived.

The law suit starts when a creditor or his lawyer writes some words on a piece of paper (known as a complaint), takes the paper to the Court Clerk, pays a filing fee, and then gives a copy of the papers to you (known as a service of process). The words that are used are much the same in most cases as form complaints are used. Only the name of the creditor and the defendant (that's you), the dates, subject of dispute, and amounts owed are changed.

A. RECEIVING THE COMPLAINT

The defendant (debtor) must be served with papers telling him what the plaintiff (creditor) is upset about. In Small Claims Court this is done either by handing the papers to the defendant, or by sending them to him via certified or registered mail. In Municipal or Superior Court the rules of service are a little stricter. Here the defendant must be handed the papers personally or, if he can't be located, the papers may be handed to a person at least 18 years of age at the defendant's home or business and another copy mailed to the defendant. There are other ways that a person can be served depending on the type of action (sometimes including publication in a newspaper). If you want to understand the technicalities of service go to a law library and check California Code of Civil Procedure Sections 413.10-417.30. Once issued by a court, papers must be served on you within three years to be valid. (C.C.P. 581a.) Once served, the plaintiff has an additional three years in which to get a judgment if you fail to respond. If he doesn't, the case shall be dismissed. (C.C.P. 581a.)

B. WHICH COURT ARE YOU BEING SUED IN?

Where you are sued depends primarily on the amount of money in dispute:

1. Small Claims Court— disputes involving $750 or less, or where a creditor with a claim larger than $750 decides to permanently give up his claim to all amounts over $750. No one is required to use Small Claims Court. A $200 case, for example, could be started in either Small Claims or Municipal Court.

2. Justice Court—exists only in rural areas, where Municipal Courts and Small Claims Courts have not been set up. Creditors can sue for **$15,000 or less.**

3. Municipal Courts—disputes involving $15,000 or less.

4. Superior Court—disputes involving $15,000 or more.

C. READING THE COMPLAINT

Small Claims Court complaints are easy to read. The amount in dispute and the reason for the debt are both clearly stated. Complaints filed in Municipal or Superior Court are often harder to figure out as they are full of legal jargon. Don't be intimidated,

---

* Under experimental legislation the Small Claims Court maximum has been raised to $1500 in the Oakland-Piedmont, Compton, East Los Angeles, West Orange County, San Bernardino (Chino division) and Fresno judicial districts.

most of the words are not important. Sometimes complaints are divided into sections called "Causes of Action." This normally means that you are being sued for more than one thing in the same complaint. All you really need to know is:

1. Who is suing you;
2. The reason for the suit;
3. How much you are being sued for;
4. The court you are being sued in.

On the first page you will be told the name of the Court and the name of the person suing. This person is called the plaintiff and his name appears at the top of the box on the first page.

Michael Millemann, Atty.
11 Betsy Street
San Francisco, California

SUPERIOR COURT OF CALIFORNIA,
COUNTY OF SAN FRANCISCO

John The Loan Shark,
    Plaintiff,

    vs.   COMPLAINT

Pancho Elliston,   No. 7015
    Defendant.

Sometimes the person suing (the plaintiff) will not be a name you recognize. This may be because the original creditor has sold the account to the plaintiff. This is legal, but if it has been done, it must be so stated in one of the first few numbered paragraphs.

Read through all the paragraphs to find out what the plaintiff claims the money is owed for. This usually appears in the middle and is often surrounded by a bunch of legal jargon, but if you slow down and read carefully you will figure it out. To find out the total amount owed, look at the last page of the complaint for the word WHEREFORE in capital letters. Here it states the total amount that the creditor claims you owe.

D. IF YOU FEEL YOU OWE THE MONEY

In a great many cases where a debtor is sued, the money is properly owed. In this situation you can proceed in one or more of the following ways:

1. Do Nothing. If you fail to respond to the complaint, you will automatically lose the case and a judgment will be taken against you for the amount set out in the complaint, plus court costs and attorney fees if there was a credit agreement calling for them. Once the creditor gets the judgment he can go after your bank account, wages, or property (see chapters 10, 11 and 12). Of course this is nothing to worry about if you are judgment proof (see chapter 1), or if you plan to file bankruptcy (see chapter 18).

2. Call the creditor and try to make a settlement. In chapter 7 we discuss this procedure. If you offer to pay cash, the creditor will normally accept considerably less than the total. Also he will often be willing to waive attorney fees or greatly reduce them.

3. See an attorney and have him do the negotiating for you. By threatening bankruptcy, indicating that he may oppose the suit or just generally knowing how to throw sand in the air, an attorney can probably make a settlement for far less than the total debt. Of course, this approach depends on your having enough money to pay the settlement amount (see chapter 3).

E. IF YOU FEEL YOU HAVE A DEFENSE

1. Small Claims Court

If you are sued in Small Claims Court, you need file no written response. Just show up on the day of the hearing and tell your story to the judge. This is the time to bring letters, photographs, and witnesses. No lawyers are allowed either side and the proceedings are fairly informal. See chapter 2, section B, and get a copy of **Everybody's Guide to Small Claims Court** (see back of this book). If you lose, you may request that the judge allow you to pay off the debt with small monthly payments.

2. Municipal Or Superior Court

If you are sued in Municipal or Superior Court, you must file a **written** answer in the correct form within 30 days from the time the papers are served on you. At this point you would be wise to consult an attorney if you are able to do so (see chapter 3). The creditor will win the case by default if no written answer is filed within the 30 days. Unless you file legal papers to set aside the judgment right away and give the court a valid reason, such as illness, for failing to respond within the first thirty days, the judgment will be final and unchangeable. Normally you will need an attorney to do this. You had your chance to tell your story to the judge, and you blew it.

You can, of course, represent yourself in Municipal or Superior Court if you can't, or don't want to pay a lawyer and are not eligible for legal aid. This means that you would file your own answer and then appear in court by yourself. We know many people who have successfully advocated their own cases and we are very supportive of the idea that courts should welcome everyone. But we want to remind you that courts are very technical and difficult for many non-lawyers to deal with. Also, some judges simply do not give non-lawyers (especially low-income people) the respect that is given lawyers. Also, the plaintiffs may be more likely to make a favorable "deal" with your lawyer than with you, since they believe that a lawyer will be better able to handle the matter in court. It is a sad commentary on our laws and civilization that it is so difficult for ordinary folks to speak for themselves, especially when you consider that it need not be this way.

If you still want to go ahead and represent yourself, it is your right to do so. Many others have managed it very successfully. We are only going to show you how to file a simple answer which will get you into court. You may have other remedies, but they are beyond the scope of this book. If you desire to defend your case in a more sophisticated manner, making legal motions and raising affirmative defenses, go to a law library and ask to see **California Forms, California Practice** and **California Jurisprudence** (third edition). Look in the index under the subjects that interest you. These books contain information and authorities on various concepts of law and possible defenses, with copies of the relevant laws and useful forms. If you have trouble, ask the law librarian for help.

Your answer must be filed within 30 days after you are served with court papers (if the 30th day falls on a weekend or holiday, you may file on the next business day). The answer should be typed (original and 3 copies on numbered 8½" by 11" paper (available at any stationery store). It should look like the illustration on the following pages.

It is important that the answer be signed by **all** of the defendants whose names appear on the complaint. The verification need only be signed by any one defendant. The "Declaration of Service by Mail" must be signed by someone who is **not** a defendant and who is a citizen over the age of 18.

After you prepare your Answer and Declaration, have one copy mailed to the creditor's lawyer (or, if he has none, to the creditor) and keep the other copies. Take the original to the office of the Clerk of the court in which the complaint was filed. To file it, you will have to pay a filing fee. How much this is depends on how many defendants there are. It will probably be between $25 and $60.

Sometime after you file your answer, you will receive a piece of paper entitled "Memorandum that civil case is at issue." This is prepared by the attorney for the creditor and is sent to the court, with a copy to you, as notice that the case is ready for trial. Eventually (sometimes it's only a few weeks and sometimes it's months, depending on how busy the court is) you will receive a notice from the clerk of the court telling you when the

---

* Many people have difficulty figuring out how to use a law library. Like so much else to do with law, information is hidden by use of a code that only the initiated understand. To break the code, see Gilberts, *Legal Research,* Honigsberg, or *How to Find and Understand the Law,* by Elias, Nolo Press.

trial will be held. On the day of the trial, make sure you show up on time, ready to prove your case, **with any witnesses you have.** (Letters or other documents will probably not be accepted unless they are to or from the creditor or his agent. You must have "live testimony."

When you get to trial, here are some of the possible defenses you might raise if they fit your case and if you can prove them:

1. You never received the goods or services that the creditor claims he provided;

2. The goods or services provided you were seriously defective;

3. As part of the delivering of the goods or services the creditor damaged your property or possessions;

4. You were charged excessive interest;

5. Serious misrepresentations were made by the creditor to get you to sign in the first place.

F. LEGAL FEES AND COURT COSTS

No one has any right to legal fees unless there is a contract stating that in the event of a law suit, legal fees can be recovered. This is included in almost all written credit contracts.* Normally legal fees in debt collection cases run to 20-25 percent of the total debt. Of course, legal fees are recoverable only by the person who wins the case. Where there is a contract provision saying that the creditor can recover legal fees if he sues you, California law says that you are entitled to collect your attorney fees from the creditor if you win the law suit. This is true even though the credit agreement only states the creditor's right to attorney fees.

Court costs (filing fee and fee for service of process) are always added to a judgment and recoverable by the winner whether or not there is any written agreement. These costs may run as low as $5 in Small Claims Court and will average $25-$75 in Municipal or Superior Court.

---

* Where a collection agency handles a debt that is not based on a written contract they will try to get you to sign one. They do this by acting sweet and reasonable when you ask for lower payments, but only if you will sign a contract. The contract, of course provides for attorney fees. Be especially careful whenever you see the Big Bad Wolf pretending to be Little Red Riding Hood. This is when he is most dangerous.

```
 1   Your name _____
 2       Address _____
 3               _____
 4       Phone _____
 5   Defendant, in pro per
 6
 7
 8
 9              MUNICIPAL COURT OF THE STATE OF CALIFORNIA
10
11
12   _____,
13              Plaintiff(s)        No. ____
14        vs.
15   _____,                      ANSWER
16              Defendant(s)
17
18              Defendant(s) answer the complaint as follows:
19
20                              I
21          Admit the allegations contained in paragraph(s) _____ , _____ ,
22   and _____ [of the 1st Cause of Action, and paragraph(s) _____ ,
23   _____ and _____ of the 2d Cause of Action].
24
25                              II
26          With the exception of the admisisons set forth above, defendant(s) deny
27   each and every, all and singular, generally and specifically the allegations
28   contained in paragraph(s) _____ , _____ and _____ [of the 1st Cause
29   of Action, and paragraphs _____ , _____ and _____ of the 2d Cause
30   of Action].
31
32          WHEREFORE Defendant(s) pray that Plaintiff(s) take nothing by this
```

action; that defendant(s) recover costs of suit including reasonable attorneys fees; and for such other relief as may be deemed just.

⑥ ⟶ _____
Defendant

_____
Defendant

VERIFICATION

I am (a) defendant in the above action; I have read the foregoing Answer, and know the contents thereof; and I certify that the same is true of my own knowledge.

I certify, under penalty of perjury, that the foregoing is true and correct.

Executed on _____[date]_____, 197__, at _____[place]_____, California.

⑦ ⟶ _____
Defendant

PROOF OF SERVICE BY MAIL

I am a citizen of the United States and a resident of the county of _____, I am over the age of 18 years and not a party to the above action; my residence address is: _____, California. On_____, 197__, I served the within Answer on the Plaintiffs in said action by placing a true copy thereof enclosed in a sealed envelope with postage thereon fully prepaid, in the United States post office mail box at_____[city]_____, California, addressed as follows: ⟵ ⑧

_____

I, ____[name of sender]____, certify under penalty of perjury that the foregoing is true and correct. Executed on ____[date]____, 197__, at____[city], California.

⑨ ⟶ _____
[signature]

NOTES

1. Type in the title of the court, exactly as it appears on the Complaint.

2. Type in the names of the parties, exactly as it appears on the Complaint.

3. Don't forget to type in the number of the case. Get it from the Complaint.

4. Read the Complaint very carefully and type in here the number of each paragraph which you can agree with completely. Do not list here any paragraph which has anything in it with which you do not agree. If there is more than one Cause of Action in the Complaint, continue as shown by the words within the parentheses.

5. Type in the number of each paragraph of the Complaint which has anything in it with which you do not agree. Use the words in the parentheses if there is more than one cause of action.

6. The Answer must be signed by each person who has been named as a Defendant in the Complaint and who has been legally served, because any person who doesn't sign has not answered and may lose by default.

7. Any one of the defendants can sign the Verification. Type in the date and place where signed.

8. Enter here the name of the creditor or his attorney, as it appears in the upper left of the first page of the Complaint.

9. Signature of person mailing Answer to plaintiffs.

G. THE JUDGMENT

Once a judgment has been entered against you, whether you defaulted or you went to court and lost the case, the creditor can move to collect on it. You may appeal the decision to a higher court. In most cases it is usually not worth the considerable cost of doing this. Appeal courts normally, but by no means always, agree with the decision of the lower court. If you decide to appeal, you will need an attorney (see chapter 3).

Once the creditor has a judgment he can attach up to 25% of your wages,* your bank account, your personal property not exempt under California law (cars, boats, and other large items of property are the things creditors go after), and your house or mobile home. In most of these areas there are practical steps by which you can protect yourself. These are discussed in chapters 9, 10, 11 and 12. Of course, if you are judgment proof or if the creditor can't find you, he can't attach anything. Bankruptcy works to wipe out almost all judgments (see Chapter 18).

H. INTEREST ON JUDGMENTS

The legal rate of interest on final judgments is 7% per year in California. This is true even if the rate of interest on the debt that was sued on was more than 7% (i.e., bank credit cards are usually 18%). It is also true even if there was not interest on the underlying bill (a doctor or dentist's bill). Interest is payable whether the debt is owed to the original creditor or a collection agency.

---

* Up to 50% for child and spousal support debts.

CHAPTER 9

WHEN THERE IS A JUDGMENT AGAINST YOU

Once a creditor gets a judgment against you, the law allows him additional rights in trying to collect it. As a "judgment creditor," he can direct the sheriff or marshall in your county to go after your possessions, any money you have in the bank, and up to 25% of your earnings. (All these things make up your "assets.")[*] He can continue his efforts to collect until he recovers the debt plus court costs and often attorney's fees. He has 10 years to collect on his judgment and he can usually get an extension for an additional 10 years.

This procedure is usually known as "Attachment" and to make it as clear as possible we have divided our discussion into three separate chapters. The first is on wages, usually the first asset a judgment creditor goes after. The second chapter will be on "personal" property which includes most of the things you own, like your motor vehicle, bank account, furniture, clothes, etc. The third chapter will cover "real" property which is just a fancy legal term for your house and land.

Just as every coin has two sides, the flip side to the

---

[*]Up to 50% for child and spousal support debts.

attachment procedure is the law on "exempt assets." Long ago the State decided that the debtor should not have to lose everything just because he owes money. After all, he still has to eat, keep a roof over his head, and provide for his family. In recognition of this, the legislature has made many assets "exempt" from attachment. Some people who don't have a lot of possessions to start with may find that most things they own are exempt.

The following three chapters will discuss which assets of yours are exempt. Here is one thing you should know now—in order to take advantage of the law, you must file a "Claim of Exemption." If a judgment creditor attaches an asset of yours which under the law would be exempt and you do not file a "Claim of Exemption" in time, you lose the asset—Poof! Enough said for now. Instructions and forms for Claims of Exemption will be covered in these chapters as they become necessary.

IMPORTANT—Federal and State tax collectors can attach wages, bank accounts, personal property and real property without getting a judgment. Claims of exemptions are allowed against state tax claims but not against federal ones. (See chapter 16.)

CHAPTER 10

WAGE ATTACHMENTS

If you haven't yet done so, read chapter 9.

Your pay check is usually the first asset a judgment creditor goes after.* It is easy to find and profitable to attach. The procedure is commonly called a "Wage Attachment," even though the correct term is "Wage Garnishment."

A. HOW MUCH CAN YOU LOSE?

Except for child support or spousal payments or taxes, no more than 25% of your net earnings (after tax, and social security deductions) can be attached.** If your net earnings are low, even less or nothing may be taken. The chart on the next page shows you the maximum amounts that can be attached.

---

* If you work on commission, the commissions you receive are considered wages and can be attached in the same manner as wages.

** Your wages may be attached from 50% (see Chapter 17) on child support and spousal support payments and 50% on state tax payments. The federal tax people can take it all if they want, but usually don't in hardship situations.

ONE-WEEK PAY PERIOD

Net Earnings*	Withhold
$1.00 to $100.50	Nothing
$100.51 to $134.00	All over $100.50
$134.01 and up	25%

TWO-WEEK PAY PERIOD

Net Earnings*	Withhold
$1.00 to $201.00	Nothing
$201.01 to $268.00	All over $201.00
$268.01 and up	25%

SEMI-MONTHLY PAY PERIOD

Net Earnings*	Withhold
$1.00 to $217.75	Nothing
$217.76 to $290.33	All over $217.75
$290.34 and up	25%

MONTHLY PAY PERIOD

Net Earnings*	Withhold
$1.00 to $435.50	Nothing
$435.51 to $580.67	All over $435.50
$580.68 and up	25%

* after tax and social security deductions

This chart is based on the federal minimum wage law which, as of January 1, 1981 is $3.35 per hour. The minimum wage may very likely rise in future years. As it does, the amounts in the chart will similarly rise. You can probably find out these new amounts by calling the sheriff or marshal's office in your county—or go to a bookstore or library, look for a later edition of this book and just copy out the new figures.

B. THE WAGE ATTACHMENT PROCEDURE—HOW IT WORKS

1. A creditor has sued you on a debt and gotten a judgment against you. He is now a "judgment creditor."

2. Often immediately, but any time within the next ten years, assuming that the judgment creditor knows where you work, he can get an order from the court allowing him to attach your wages. This is called a "Writ of Execution."

3. He takes the "writ" to the sheriff or marshall, pays a fee, and instructs him to attach your wages as described in the "writ."

4. The sheriff visits your employer, serves him a copy of the "writ" and instructs him to withhold up to 25% of your net earnings. Your employer must send the amount he withholds at each pay period to the sheriff. The sheriff will deduct his expenses and give the remainder to the judgment creditor.

5. As soon as the sheriff notifies your employer of the attachment, the sheriff must also notify you.

C. BEING FIRED FOR A WAGE ATTACHMENT

Often employers consider wage attachments to be a big hassle and just too much paperwork (now that most checks are made out by computer) to deduct the 25% of your net earnings each pay period and send it to the sheriff. Therefore, some will pressure the employee to settle the debt right away or be fired.

Well, under federal law, an employer can **not** fire you for the garnishment of **one** debt. This means that no matter how often a judgment creditor attaches your earnings, if it is only for one debt, you cannot be fired. But, if two judgment creditors attach your wages with the same employer, whether at the same or different times, you can be fired. Also, if one judgment creditor attaches your wages for two different debts, you can be fired.

Now, what may happen is that even though a judgment creditor attaches your wages for only one debt, your employer

97

gets antsy and wants the matter settled. He knows he cannot fire you because of one attachment. But he may fire you for some phony reason such as being late to work. If this should happen, see a lawyer right away. If you are poor, legal aid can help you.

We have found, however, that most employers are willing to work with employees who are honestly trying to clear up their problems. It is best to talk with your employer when your wages are being attached and make him understand that you are working hard to settle the matter as soon as possible.

D. STOPPING A WAGE ATTACHMENT

1. Negotiation

Creditors attach your wages because they cannot get money from you any other way. They don't particularly like the paper work involved and are afraid that a wage attachment may result 'n your filing bankruptcy or perhaps even getting fired. So, they will normally agree to stop an attachment if you make some reasonable offer of payment. It's never too late to begin negotiating with them. They have more clout now, but you can still work out an agreement. Go back and read chapter 7.

You should also consider contacting Consumer Credit Counsellors (see chapter 3, section C). They carry considerable weight and often can persuade the judgment creditor to halt the attachment and work out an agreement.

2. Bankruptcy

Filing bankruptcy will end the wage attachment. But before you decide to file, read chapter 18.

3. Claim Of Exemption

You can exempt from attachment **whatever portion** of your

income is necessary for the support of yourself and/or your family. If you are living with your spouse or supporting parents or children who reside in California (whether or not they live with you), this would constitute a family.

NOTE—The debt cannot be for a common necessity of life. This is something which is universally recognized as necessary for everyone. Thus, common necessities would be items like the following (not a complete list):

> rent
> food
> utilities
> most clothes (but not luxury items)
> medical bills (but not necessarily psychiatrist bills)
> beds and basic furniture

They would not be:

> restaurant bills
> veterinary bills
> automobiles
> motor cycles
> garden equipment
> fancy furniture
> boats
> sports equipment
> cameras
> travel

If your debt is not for a "common necessary" or if there is any confusion on whether it would be one, you should file your claim of exemption. It shouldn't be hard for you to show the judge that you need the income for support of yourself and family.

Many attorneys feel you should always file your claim of exemption even if the debt is clearly for a "common necessary." They say this because there will be times when the judgment creditor will not challenge your claim and you will win automatically. Also, some judges do not consider whether the debt is for a common necessity—they just see whether you can afford to pay the debt or not.

a. How The Claim Of Exemption Procedure Works

1. You should file your claim of exemption as soon as possible after you receive an "earnings withholding order"* from your employer. Your employer must provide you with a copy of this order within 10 days of the time he or she receives it.

2. After you file your claim of exemption and an accompanying "financial statement," the judgment creditor is notified and he has 10 days to file a challenge to the claim. Most of the time he or she will contest, but sometimes because of the costs, he or she may decide to abandon it. If the judgment creditor doesn't follow through, your withheld wages will be returned to you.

3. If he does contest it, you will be notified and a hearing date will be set before a judge. The hearing will probably be a week or two later, depending upon the county. Make certain you show up. If you don't, you will lose by default. At the hearing you will have to show that you need your earnings for the support of yourself and/or your family, and that the item on which you owe the money is not a common necessity of life (see D3 above).

4. The judge will hear both sides and then make a ruling. Often he or she will agree with you that the item is not a common necessity, and that all your earnings are necessary and should be exempt. But sometimes the judge will try to work out a compromise and make you pay something. (There are judges who feel that a debtor should never be allowed to "skip" on his/her debts.)

5. If you win at the hearing, the judgment creditor must wait at least 100 days from the date the earnings withholding order was first served on your employer or 60 days from the date of your hearing, whichever is later, before he or she can attach your wages again. If a compromise results or if you lose, then the judgment creditor can attach your wages in the amount settled on for 90 days or until the debt is paid off.

6. After 90 days, the judgment creditor must wait ten days before he or she can file a new earnings withholding order. You can then file another claim of exemption against the new attachment.

---

* The law on wage attachment is found in the Code of Civil Procedure, Sections 723.010 et. seq.

b. Filing Your Claim Of Exemption

The procedure for filling out a claim of exemption is fairly simple. If you feel confident in yourself, you can probably do it without a lawyer. Judges are getting used to people doing their own Claim of Exemption. However, judges often prefer to deal with lawyers rather than people themselves. So it often happens that if you appear at a claim of exemption hearing alone, you will more likely be drawn into a compromise with the judgment creditor than if you have a lawyer representing you. If you have a low income, call legal aid. If you intend to do it yourself, here's what you should do.

1. The employer must give you a copy of the "earnings withholding order" he or she received within ten days from the day he or she received it.

2. As soon as you receive it, you should go down to the sheriff, marshal or constable's office to file your claim of exemption. There is no time limit on when you must file, but if you want to keep as much as you possibly can, you should file your claim right away. (If for some reason you cannot file until later, the judge has the power to retroactively reduce the amount of wages the judgment creditor can take from you.)

3. Your county sheriff, marshal or constable's office and possibly also the clerk of the court listed on top of the notice you received will have the proper "claim of exemption" and "financial statement" forms which you must fill out.

4. You file the original and one copy each of the claim of exemption and the financial statement with the sheriff, marshal or constable. Make a copy of each for yourself too. If you have trouble filling out the form, ask the clerk at the sheriff, marshal or constable's office or at the court to assist you.

5. Within a couple of weeks, you will be notified whether the judgment creditor intends to contest your claim. If he does, you will be told of the date of the hearing and the court room (called a "department"). **Make sure you appear.** If you do not, you will lose your claim.

If the judgment creditor does not intend to contest your claim, you will so be notified and have your wages returned to you.

6. On the day of your hearing, come early. Check with the court clerk to be sure you are in the right room. Relax and watch the way the judge handles other cases. (If you are nervous, visit the court a day earlier just to get yourself accustomed to the surroundings.)

7. At the hearing, you will have to prove your claim. You should be prepared to argue that you need your income to support yourself and/or your family. If you have made an unusually high income one month, bring wage stubs and other proof to show that you usually make much less. Also, if you have unusually high medical bills one month, bring proof. The judge is not required to look at these proofs, but he probably will.

Most judges are used to people doing it themselves, so don't be frightened. Tell him how serious it would be if you weren't allowed to keep all your income. He may try to draw you into agreeing to pay something, so be prepared. If you're suffering, let him know it. If you have kids, bring them along and let them sit in the first row. Remember, the judge is not going to know how much you are hurting unless you tell him.

8. Good luck.

c. How Often Can You File A Claim Of Exemption - Have Your Circumstances Changed?

You can file a claim of exemption against a wage attachment anytime after you receive the "earnings withholding order." See section a6 above. Once you file your claim, unless your circumstances have changed, you must wait until you receive a new earnings withholding order (usually within 100 days from the last) before you can file another claim of exemption.

However, if your circumstances have changed (for example, you have additional medical expenses or increased support payments, or your rent has gone up, etc.), you can immediately file at anytime for another claim of exemption.

d. Legislation To Automatically Protect People's Rights

If you have only had to read the wage exemption material three times to understand it, you are doing pretty well. Yes, it's needlessly complicated and cumbersome. But you should understand that the complications exist not because they need to, but because creditors want debtors to have to go to so much trouble to exempt their wages that they won't bother. What can you do? Contact your state legislator and request legislation to do away with these unfair procedures which make a person in debt rush to file legal papers in order to keep the money he or she desperately needs.

ATTORNEY OR PARTY WITHOUT ATTORNEY (Name and Address)	TELEPHONE NO	LEVYING OFFICER (Name and Address)

ATTORNEY FOR (Name)

Name of court, judicial district or branch court, if any

PLAINTIFF

DEFENDANT

CLAIM OF EXEMPTION AND FINANCIAL DECLARATION	LEVYING OFFICER FILE NUMBER	COURT CASE NUMBER

READ THE EMPLOYEE INSTRUCTIONS BEFORE COMPLETING THIS FORM.

Copy the information required above from the Earnings Withholding Order. The top left space is for your or your attorney's name and address.

1. I need the following earnings to support myself or my family (check a. or b.):
   a. ☐ All earnings.   b. ☐ $ . . . . each pay period.

2. Please send all paper to ☐ me ☐ my attorney at the address ☐ shown above ☐ following (specify):

3. I am willing for the following amount to be withheld from my earnings during the withholding period. **I understand that the judgment creditor can accept this offer by not opposing the Claim of Exemption, which will result in the following sum being withheld each pay period:**

   ☐ None   ☐ Withhold $ . . . . each pay period.

4. a. I am paid ☐ daily ☐ weekly ☐ every two weeks ☐ twice a month ☐ monthly.

   b. My gross pay is $ . . . . per pay period.

   c. My take-home pay is $ . . . . per pay period.

   d. List payroll deductions (item and amount):

5. The following persons depend, in whole or in part, on me for support:

NAME	AGE	THEIR RELATIONSHIP TO ME	THEIR MONTHLY INCOME AND ITS SOURCE
a.		Myself	
b.			
c.			
d.			
e.			

6. The earnings of others listed in item 5 are now subject to wage assignments and Earnings Withholding Orders as follows (specify):

(Continued on reverse)

Form Adopted by the Judicial Council of California Effective January 1, 1980	**CLAIM OF EXEMPTION AND FINANCIAL DECLARATION (Wage Garnishment)**	CCP 723 105 (b) 723 124

(front)

7. MY MONTHLY EXPENSES ARE:

a. Rent or house payment
and maintenance . . . . $. . . . . . .

b. Food and household supplies . . . $. . . . . .

c. Utilities and telephone . . . . $. . . . . .

d. Clothing. . . . . $. . . . . .

e. Laundry & cleaning . . . . $. . . . .

f. Medical and dental payments . . . $. . . . .

g. Insurance (life, health,
accident, etc.) . . . . $. . . . . .

h. School, child care . . . . $. . . . . . .

i. Child. spousal support
(prior marriage) . . . . $. . . . . .

j. Entertainment, incidentals . . . . . $. . . . .

k. Transportation & auto expenses
(insurance, gas, repair) . . . . $. . . . .

l. Installment payments (Insert
total and itemize below at 8) . . . . $. . . . .

m. Other (specify): . . . . $. . . . .

TOTAL MONTHLY EXPENSES . $
(add a. through m.)

8. List payments on installment and other debts. ☐Continued on attachment 8.

Creditor's Name	For	Monthly Payments	Balance

9. What do you own? (State value.)

a. Cash . . . . $. . . . . .

b. Checking, savings and
credit union accounts
(list banks):
1. . . . . $. . . . . .
2. . . . . $. . . . . .
3. . . . . $. . . . . .

c. Cars, other vehicles and
boat equity (list make,
year of each):
1. . . . . $. . . . . .
2. . . . . $. . . . . .
3. . . . . $. . . . . .

d. Real estate equity
(address):
$. . . . . . .

e. Other personal property
(jewelry, furniture, furs, stocks
and bonds, etc. List separately):

$. . . . . . .

10. ☐ An order Assigning Salary and Wages (for support) is now in effect as to my earnings. The amount payable
under that order is $. . . . . monthly.

11. Other facts which support this Claim of Exemption are (describe unusual medical needs, school tuition, expenses
for recent family emergencies, or other unusual expenses to help your creditor and the judge understand your
budget). If more space is needed, attach page labelled Attachment 11.

12. I declare under penalty of perjury that the foregoing is true and correct and that this declaration is executed
on (date) . . . . at (place) . . . . , California.

. . . . (Type or print name) . . . .   _____
                                                                 (Signature of Judgment Debtor)

Deliver the original and one copy of this form to the levying officer at the address shown on the Earnings Withholding Order.

If you are signing this in California, it does not have to be notarized.

(back)

105

CHAPTER 11

ATTACHMENTS OF MOTOR VEHICLES, BANK ACCOUNTS AND OTHER PERSONAL PROPERTY

If you have not done so, read chapter 9.

Besides attaching your wages, the judgment creditor may attach your personal property. Personal property is everything but a house and land. (They are called real property and are discussed in the following chapter.)

Often a debtor does not have much in the way of valuable personal possessions and what he has is exempt; see section B below. But if he has a fairly valuable car that is paid for, furniture which can easily be resold such as a stereo component set costing $1,500, or money in the bank, etc., the judgment creditor may decide to come after it. Attachments of furniture are quite rare and only occur where there are extremely valuable items. Attachments of bank accounts and motor vehicles are common. If the judgment creditor does decide to attach, he will send the sheriff or marshall to take the item, have it sold at

public auction and apply the proceeds of the sale to the debt. The procedure is not much different from a wage attachment, but let's go through it.

A. THE ATTACHMENT PROCEDURE

1. The judgment creditor has just gotten a judgment against you on the debt.

2. Often immediately, but any time within the next 10 years he can get an order from the court allowing him to attach your property. This is called a "writ of execution."

3. He pays the sheriff a fee and instructs him to attach the asset of yours which is described in the "writ." Since a car is often the most common possession attached, let's use it for our example. Other personal property is treated in a similar way.

4. The sheriff or marshall goes out to your home (or wherever the judgment creditor says your car is located). If you are home, he will explain that he has come to take the car in order to sell it and use the proceeds of the sale to pay off part or all of your debt. If you are not home, he will post the writ on your door.

5. If you do not give him the keys, or if you are not home, he will use a master set of his own or hot wire the car. (You can be arrested for interfering with him, so stay cool.)

6. He will take the car to a garage for storage and wait 10 days.

7. If you do not file a claim of exemption on the car (see section D) within that time, he will offer the vehicle at a public sale.

8. The sale is usually held a week or two later, depending upon the county. The proceeds of the sale will be used to pay off the debt, though the sheriff will first take out his costs and towing and storage charges.

B. EXEMPT ASSETS

We mentioned in chapter 9 that the state has adopted legislation to protect you from losing all your possessions to the judgment creditor. You should not have to be without certain basic items, merely because you owe money on a debt. These items are known as "exempt assets" and most of them are personal property. Here is a list of the most common ones:

1. Household Items

These include the following:
    household furnishings

appliances

clothes

piano (but, curiously, not any other musical instrument unless it comes under number 3 below)

T.V.

radio

3 months provisions and fuel

shotgun

rifle

The law requires that the household furnishings be "necessary" and that the clothing be "ordinarily and reasonably necessary." Courts are pretty lenient in finding that almost all furniture and clothing is "necessary," but would probably draw the line at a beer bar or a mink coat. Therefore, you should always file a claim of exemption on any clothing, furniture, or appliance.

2. Motor Vehicles

You can keep one motor vehicle (automobile, truck, motorcycle) where the amount of your equity in it is worth no more than $500. To find out the sale value of the vehicle, look it up in the blue book (any public library, credit union, or used car dealer will have one). If your car is not listed in the blue book, take the average of the prices listed for the vehicle in the newspaper and subtract 15% to 20%, since these prices are often inflated. To find out your equity in the vehicle, check your payment book or call up the people you are making payments to. Subtract what you owe from the sale value of the car. If the figure you end up with is $500 or less, you can keep the vehicle. (If you are not making payments, then your equity in the vehicle is equal to the value of the vehicle.)

If your equity is more than $500, the creditor through the sheriff or bankruptcy trustee might take it, sell it at a public sale, and apply the proceeds to your debts. However, if it is sold, the purchaser must **pay you up to your $500 exemption in cash** and the amount you receive is protected from attachment for 3 months.

If you own more than one motor vehicle in which you have some equity, you will lose all but one of them unless you can include the others in number 3 below.

3. Tools Of Your Trade Or Business

You can keep $2,500 worth of tools, instruments, uniforms, books, equipment, commercial motor vehicles, and other property you use in your trade, business or profession. Farm animals and agricultural property would obviously be included here. Be imaginative.

4. Savings

You can claim an exemption for up to $1,000 in a savings and loan company and $1,500 in a credit union.* (Financial Code Section 15.406.) Note that this exception does not apply to regular savings banks or commercial banks.

5. A Housetrailer Or Mobile Home

A housetrailer, mobile home, houseboat, boat or other water-borne vessel in which you or your family resides is exempt, up to $30,000 for a single person not yet 65, and $45,000 for a head of family and for single people 65 or older. However, to use this exemption, the following must apply: 1) it must be your principal residence, 2) you or your spouse do not own a home with a homestead exemption, and 3) you have not obtained a court order that another home of yours is exempt from creditors levying on it under C.C.P. Section 690.31. See next chapter.

6. Life And Health Insurance Policies

Life and health insurance policies are exempt if the premiums (the amount you pay to the insurance company) of each do not exceed $500 a year. If the premiums are higher, they still may be exempt under a proportional method worked out by the legislature. Speak to a lawyer about this.

7. Pension And Retirement Benefits

Pension and retirement benefits are exempt. These benefits retain their exempt status if deposited in a bank, but see next paragraph.

---

*Credit unions now offer share draft accounts, which function like checking accounts in commercial banks, but qualify for the $1500 credit union exemption. Many people with debt problems are finding that having a checking account on which they can claim a $1500 exemption is a real convenience.

8. Federal And State Benefits

Federal and state benefits like public assistance—welfare, social security, veterans' benefits, worker's compensation, and unemployment compensation are exempt, except that social security benefits are not exempt from court-ordered child or spousal support payments up to 50%. Even if these benefits are deposited in a bank account, they are still exempt unless they have gotten hopelessly mixed up with other non-exempt funds. However your best bet is to keep all money in a savings and loan or credit union account if you fear attachment (see B 4 above).

There are other specialized exemptions. If you think you might have some assets which seem logically to you to be an exemption, you can go to your local library and look up the entire list of exemptions in the California Code of Civil Procedure, beginning at Section 690. (Make sure you look at the supplement in back of the book to find the latest revisions.) If you have problems with the list, you can speak to an attorney.

Some assets which you might expect to be exempt are not. These include real estate, stocks and bonds, motor vehicles worth more than $500, musical instruments (except a piano), boats, and sporting equipment. (Of course, you would be able to include some of these things if they were used in your trade or profession up to the $2,500 limitation; see number 3 in our list above.)

IMPORTANT—Exemptions And Secured Debts

There is this exception to the exemption law: If you owe money on a secured debt and the secured creditor has gotten a judgment against you for it, you cannot claim that item as an exemption, though it would otherwise qualify as one. (A secured debt is where the creditor has legal title to the item until you make all the payments on it; see chapter 5.)

Here is an example: You buy a used piano for $400 and the dealer keeps legal title to it until you pay it off. You stop making payments and the dealer gets a judgment against you for the amount you still owe. The dealer then can attach the piano and you cannot claim an exemption for it (even though it would be a valid claim of exemption against any other creditor trying to attach your piano, such as a doctor or credit card company). To keep the piano you would have to continue making payments on it.

C. TURNING NON EXEMPT ASSETS INTO EXEMPT ONES

If you have an asset which is not exempt, especially money, you would do well to convert it to an asset which is exempt before the judgment creditor has a chance to attach it. This is not only sensible, but legal. Here are a few examples:

1. You have a checking or savings account with $100 in it. Close the account and put the money in your credit union (if there is $1,400 or less in it) or in a savings and loan institution (if there is $900 or less in it), or spend it on an exempt asset like a new coat, or shoes for yourself, or bunk beds for the kids.

2. You have a canoe or motor boat, and are a carpenter. Sell the boat(s) and use the money to buy yourself some more tools that you need for your work. (As long as the total sale value of all your equipment is below $2,500, you're safe.)

3. You have a valuable collection of stamps, coins, guns, or antiques. Sell it and use the money as a down payment on a home and homestead it (see chapter 12).

4. You have two cars; your equity in one car is $450, in the other it is $300. Though both fall under the $500 limit, you can only keep one of them as exempt. Sell one or the other and use the money to prepay medical and dentist bills you expect to have next month.

D. FILING YOUR CLAIM OF EXEMPTION

After the creditor gets a judgment against you, he or she then obtains a "Writ of Execution" from the court clerk. The creditor takes this writ to the sheriff or marshal and directs them to attach some item of yours in the hope that it will be used to help pay off the debt. Where the creditor goes after an item which is exempt under the law (such as your tools of your trade or savings account in a savings and loan institution or credit union), you can file a "claim of exemption" to protect it.

The procedure for filling out a claim of exemption is fairly simple. If you feel confident in yourself, you can probably do it without a lawyer. Judges are getting used to people doing their own claim of exemption. However, judges often prefer to deal with lawyers rather than people themselves. So it often happens that if you appear at a claim of exemption hearing alone, you will more likely be drawn into a compromise with the judgment creditor than if you have a lawyer representing you. If you have a low income, call legal aid. If you intend to do it yourself, here's what you should do:

1. You must file your claim with the sheriff or marshall within 10 days from the date of attachment. With bank accounts, some sheriff departments begin counting from the date the sheriff serves the writ on the bank, while others begin on the date you are notified that the bank has paid over the money. To be safe, you should file your claim of exemption as soon as you are notified of the attachment. Also, call the sheriff or marshall's office and ask them from what date they begin counting off the 10 days.

2. Get a claim of exemption form from your sheriff or marshal's office, or from the court clerk of the court listed on the paper you were served with.

3. Below is a list of the California Code of Civil Procedure sections for the more common exemptions we discussed in section C above. You will have to fill in the proper code section in the claim of exemption form. If you are filing an exemption on an asset we haven't covered, go to your local library and look up the entire list of exemptions in the California Code of Civil Procedure, beginning at section 690. (Make sure you look at the supplement in the back of the book to find the latest revisions.)

4. You will need to make four copies, three for the sheriff or marshal's office and one for yourself. Make sure you sign each copy separately.

5. You must deliver three copies to the court, sheriff or marshal's office within the ten days. If you wish to mail them, call first to make sure the sheriff or marshal will accept them by mail. If they will, they will probably require that the copies **reach** the office within the ten day period.

6. Within a week or two, you will be notified whether the judgment creditor intends to contest your claim. If so, you will be told of the date of the hearing and the court room (called a "department"). Make sure you appear. If you do not, you will lose your claim.

If the judgment creditor does not contest your claim, the property will be released back to you.

7. On the day of the hearing, come early. Check with the court clerk to be sure you are in the right room. Relax and watch the way the judge handles other cases. (If you are nervous, visit the court a day earlier to get yourself accustomed to the surroundings.)

8. Be prepared to establish your right to your property under the law. If they are your tools of your trade or your mobile home, bring an expert witness who can testify to the fact that the value does not exceed your exemption amount. Be sure to bring whatever papers or other evidence you need (savings passbook, etc.).

9. Good luck.

CIVIL PROCEDURE CODE SECTION	ASSET
690.1	Household Items: furniture, appliances, clothes, radio, T.V., piano, fuel, shotgun, rifle
690.2	Motor Vehicle
690.3	Housetrailer or Motor Home
690.4	Tools of Your Trade or Business
690.7	Savings
690.9	Life Insurance
690.11	Disability and Health Insurance
690.15	Worker's Compensation
690.175	Unemployment Insurance Benefits
690.18	Pensions, Retirement, Disability and Death Benefits
690.19	Public Assistance
Financial Code 15406	Credit Unions

NAME AND ADDRESS OF ATTORNEY	TELEPHONE NO	FOR COURT USE ONLY

ATTORNEY FOR

Insert name of court, judicial district or branch court, if any, and post office and street address

PLAINTIFF

DEFENDANT

NOTICE OF ☐ OPPOSITION TO APPLICATION FOR RIGHT TO ATTACH ORDER
☐ CLAIM OF EXEMPTION
☐ MOTION (AFTER ISSUANCE OF WRIT) FOR CLAIM OF EXEMPTION
☐ **AND MOTION FOR CLAIM OF EXEMPTION**

CASE NUMBER

1. To plaintiff (Name):

2. You are notified that at the hearing to be held in this court and set for
Date: Time: ☐ Dept. ☐ Div. ☐ Room No.:

3. Defendant (Name):
   a. ☐ Will oppose the issuance of a right to attach order upon the following grounds (State grounds of opposition. CCP 484.060(a)):

   b. ☐ Will claim exemption ☐ move the court for an exemption from attachment of the following property
      (1) ☐ Property exempt from execution under CCP 690 et seq. (Specify code section and describe property)

(Continued on reverse side)

This notice of opposition and claim of exemption together with any supporting affidavits complying with CCP 482.040 and points and authorities shall be filed and served on the plaintiff not less than five days before the date set for the hearing. If defendant fails to file and serve this notice and supporting documents within five days of the hearing date he will be denied the right to oppose issuance of the right to attach order. (CCP 484.060(a)) If defendant fails to file and serve on plaintiff his claim of exemption of property described in plaintiff's application he may not later claim the exemption except as provided in CCP 482.100 (CCP 484.070(a)). Defendant's motion for claim of exemption based on necessities (CCP 487.020(b)) pursuant to the procedure in CCP 482.100(c) requires service of this notice of motion on plaintiff not less than three days prior to the date set for the hearing.

Form Approved by the
Judicial Council of California
Effective January 1, 1977

**NOTICE OF OPPOSITION TO RIGHT TO ATTACH
ORDER AND CLAIM OF EXEMPTION
(Attachment)**

CCP 482.100 484.010 et seq
487.010 487.020(a)(b)(c)
485.610

(front)

(2) ☐ Property which is necessary for the support of an individual defendant or the defendant's family supported in whole or in part by the defendant (CCP 487.020(b). Describe Property):

(3) ☐ Compensation paid or payable to a defendant employee by an employer for personal services performed by such employee whether denominated as wages, salary, commission, bonus, or otherwise. (CCP 487.020(c). Describe compensation):

(4) ☐ Property not subject to attachment pursuant to CCP 487.010. (Describe property).

(5) ☐ Other. (Describe property and specify grounds for exemption):

4. Defendant's affidavit supporting any factual issues and points and authorities supporting any legal issues is attached.

5. Total number of pages attached:

Dated:

        (Type or print name)   (Signature of (Attorney for) Defendant)

By: (Name and Title)

(back)

116

CHAPTER 12

PROTECTING YOUR HOME AND LAND

If you have not done so, read chapter 9.

A judgment creditor usually does not care how he gets his money, he just wants to get it. And he wants it in the easiest way expending the least effort. That is why he usually goes after your wages first. But he may decide that an even more effective route would be to attach your home if you own one. He knows that your home is probably your most valuable possession and you don't want to lose it. It often happens that merely by beginning the attachment procedure against a debtor's unprotected home, a creditor frightens the debtor into figuring out some way to pay off the debt immediately and save the home.

A. CLAIM OF EXEMPTION

Up until 1976, in order to protect your dwelling house from attachment, you had to homestead it before judgment. But an enlightened legislature determined that it was unfair to take someone's home merely because the person forgot, or perhaps did not even know, of the right to homestead. So now a debtor served with a judgment can still protect his or her home by filing for an exemption just as one can do for wages or personal property. Unfortunately this protection is not as strong as that afforded by a recorded Declaration of Homestead (see Section 5 just below).

The only requirements are that you or your family at the time of the judgment actually reside on the property and that you do not have a declared homestead on any other property in California. (See number 5 below on homesteading your house.) A mobile home which you or your family reside in is also protected by this section (C.C.P. 690.31).

1. How Much Is Protected

The present dollar amount the legislature has declared protected in a dwelling house, whether homesteaded or taken under a claim of exemption, is $45,000 for a married couple, or a single head of household or an individual over 65, and $30,000 for a single person.

A judgment creditor has nothing to attach unless your equity in the home (the amount you actually own) is greater than these amounts. This is plenty of protection for most people because the institution to which the mortgage payments are made usually owns a good chunk of the home, not leaving much equity. To understand this better see number 4 below.

2. How It works

If the judgment creditor wants to attach your home, you will be served with a notice telling you that your house is in danger of being sold to satisfy the judgment and that you may be able to protect it if you or your family now actually reside on the property and do not have a homestead somewhere else in California. But you or your spouse or your attorney **must come to a hearing in court** to show that these facts are true.

If you or your spouse fail to go to the hearing and have a good excuse, you can still have the sale of your house cancelled if you file at least five days prior to date of sale an affidavit establishing your right to keep the house. You should see an attorney immediately to make sure you have a good legal excuse for not appearing at the hearing. You will then have to appear at a second hearing.

3. What A Claim of Exemption Protects and What It Doesn't

As we have said, you must reside in the dwelling house at the time of judgment and you cannot have made a declaration of homestead on any other property in California.

Your dwelling house can be a place in the country, a house in the city, a condominium, co-operative apartment, or planned unit development. It also includes all the land you own and other buildings on it like garages, guest cottages and toolsheds.

Your exemption will not protect you from the people you owe on your mortgage (secured creditors). These people can come in and move to take your home if you fall behind in payments. This procedure is called foreclosure. It will also not protect your home if you owe federal taxes and the government wants to attach your house to collect.

4. If Your Equity Is Larger Than The
Dollar Value of The Exemption Protection

If your equity in your home is larger than the $30,000 or $45,000 protection, your judgment creditor may decide to attach your home. If so, he must pay for the cost of the sale of your home, pay off all loans secured by the property (usually mortgages and trust deeds) and pay you the amount protected by your exemption. The creditor can only keep what is left over. Thus, practically speaking, your equity in the home must be quite a bit more than your protected exemption amount before a creditor will attach

If your creditor does attach your home, and it is protected by law, he must pay you the protected amount. If you use these proceeds for the purchase of another dwelling house in which you or your family will reside within six months from the time you receive the proceeds, you can continue to keep your protection in your new home.

5. Homesteading Your House

You can avoid the worry of going to a court hearing to establish your exemption on your dwelling house when a judgment creditor wants to attach it by filing a "Declaration of Homestead". You merely file a simple form with the County Recorder at any time as long as it is before someone gets a judgment against you. The homestead procedure, complete with forms necessary to file, is available in a paperback book, **Protect Your Home,** by Warner, Sherman and Ihara.

The homestead protection is identical in amount to that you get under your exemption claim, namely, $45,000 for a married couple, or a single person head of household or a person over 65, and $30,000 for a single person. It covers the same types of property that a claim of exemption does. See number 3 above.

There are several advantages in filing for a homestead protection instead of waiting until you can claim your exemption as discussed just above.

1. You do not have to be residing in the house at the time of judgment as you must with a claim of exemption. You only have to reside there at the time you file the declaration of homestead.

2. A homestead protects your equity in a home as to debts incurred prior to buying a house as long as the homestead was filed before a lien was filed against the house, but Section 690.31 does not.

3. If you sell a homestead house and your homestead was filed before any judgment liens were filed, you can get your money out of the house and have six months to put it into another house. If you have not homesteaded and liens have been filed against your home, Section 690.31 would seem to give you the same right to get your money out of one house and into another. In practice it does not, because the title companies interpret the law in a conservative fashion and will not establish clear title until you have paid off all the liens. This means that it will be difficult, or more likely impossible to sell a non-homesteaded house unless you pay all of your debts.

4. In several other areas of the law such as bankruptcy, divorce and even in regards to the definition of "dwelling house," it is not clear that an exemption under Section 690.31 gives as good protection as a homestead.

Remember, you can only homestead your house before the creditor gets a judgment and records it with the County Recorder. You can file for it while you are being sued. Homesteading will not protect you from judgments gotten against you before you filed your declaration of homestead.

B. IF YOUR HOME IS ATTACHED AND SOLD: HOW TO GET IT BACK

If your home is attached by a nasty creditor and sold at a forced sale, you still have a chance to get it back. Under the law, you may recover the property from the person who purchased it any time within 12 months from the date of sale. You must pay the amount of the purchase plus an additional charge of less than 1% per month plus taxes, maintenance and other normal costs.

This procedure is known as "Redemption." Many problems can arise in redeeming your property such as determining the precise amount you are obligated to pay and the value of any rents on the property. If you are considering redemption, you would be wise to consult a lawyer.

C. PROPERTY TAXES

California law allows you to be delinquent in your property taxes for up to five years before the property is taken and sold for back taxes. Here's an example:

If you do not pay your 1982-83 property taxes (taxes run on a fiscal year, July 1 - June 30), then on July 1, 1983 you will be considered delinquent. But not until July 1, 1988 will your property be "tax deeded" to the county and prepared for public auction in the following October. In October 1988 you would lose your property if you still hadn't paid the taxes.

You can pay delinquent property taxes any time during the five years. However, very high interest rates are added on for late payment.

If five years have passed and your property is taken by the County, you have additional time to recover it. Between July 1 and the auction in October, you can redeem your property if you pay the full amount.

There is another angle you should consider, though, when you don't pay property taxes. In some cases, the mortgager will pay the taxes and then go against you for them. This can happen anytime within the five years.

1. Are You Buying Property?

Property taxes run against property, not against people. So be careful when you purchase property. If there is a tax delinquency on it and you purchase the property, you are responsible for the delinquency.

2. Senior Citizens' Property Tax Relief

Senior citizens 62 years or older, whose income is $26,800 or less (this figure is adjusted upwards for inflation each year), can have their property taxes, special assessments and other charges and fees deferred. The amounts would be deducted from the value of their property after they die. Rev. & Tax Code Section 20581-85 and 20601 et seq. For more information call the State Controller's Office at [800] 952-5661.

D. REFINANCING AND SECOND MORTGAGES

1. Refinancing

Ten years ago Steven Mitchell bought a $30,000 home, $5,000 down and a $25,000 mortgage payable over 25 years. He has paid off $10,000 to date. Today he is in debt and needs money. To get it, he can "refinance" his home. He would take a new mortgage (possibly again $25,000) on his home, use it to pay off what is left on his present mortgage ($15,000) and pocket the difference ($10,000).*

Turning in your equity in your home for cash is sometimes a good idea. But if you intend to do it, consider the following:

a) It will extend the time period in which you have to pay off the mortgage and make it harder for you to ever own your home "free and clear."

b) If interest rates are high, it will cost you more to pay off your home than if you continued paying at the rate you got at the time you took the original mortgage.

c) Always go to a bank or credit union first. Be sure to check with the people who have the original mortgage and find out how much of a pre-payment penalty you incur by paying off the mortgage ahead of time. Shop around for the best terms.

d) If the equity in your home is climbing above the dollar value of the homestead exemption, you can refinance your home and bring that equity down, so your creditors will not have anything to attach.

2. Second Mortgages

In our above example, Steven could also go to a second mortgage company (they often have the word "plan" as a part of their name), borrow $10,000, and mortgage his house as a security for the loan. This would be his "second mortgage."

People often take second mortgages rather than refinance their home. Usually this is a bad choice. Whenever possible, you should refinance. It will save you a lot of headaches and possible misery.

---

* With today's inflated prices of homes, Steven's old home would probably be worth over $125,000. Thus he could refinance his home for a lot more (perhaps even up to $110,000) and walk away with a huge bundle.

Here's how second mortgage companies operate:

Most real estate "plans" which offer second mortgages are nothing more than "mortgage brokers" who use the money of rich people who want to invest in high interest paying loans. The brokers rarely invest their own money.

The interest rate is 12%–18% and there are a number of additional charges like "finder's fees" or commissions, title insurance, title search, credit investigations, and escrow and recording fees. This can all total up to a whopping 29% of the loan.

On loans for 3 years or more, many of these companies provide for the final installment payment to be much greater than the preceding installment payments. This final payment is called a "balloon payment." Often people are unable to make this payment and so are forced to refinance and again pay all those costs, commissions, expenses, etc. So watch out.

These groups advertise that they are not interested in your credit. They will lend you the money no matter how bad your credit. Sounds attractive. But it isn't. Remember, you put up your home as security. And if you miss a payment—zoom—they swoop down and take it from you. They often hope that people will not repay. They make their big profits in foreclosing on your home and milking all the equity you have in it.

Some collection agencies are in cohoots with these "plans." When you owe collection agencies money, they may suggest you take a second mortgage with a "plan" which they name. Watch out. They may have a kickback deal going with the plan. Don't take the "friendly" advice of the collection agency. They are not your friends. Check for the best refinancing or second mortgage deal on your own.

a. Checking Out A "Plan"

If your bank or credit union will not refinance your home and you need to go to one of these "plans" to get a second mortgage, call the Better Business Bureau. Ask them on which second mortgage "plans" they have received complaints. Don't go to these. Some brokers are more reputable than others. Check around.

124

b. Making A Complaint

If you have any trouble with any of these plans or brokers or salesmen, contact the Department of Real Estate office that covers your area. (Let the plan know that you are complaining.) There are offices in Sacramento, San Francisco, Fresno, Los Angeles, and San Diego. The addresses and phone numbers are listed below. You can make a complaint in person (bring all important papers with you) or call and ask them to send you a complaint form, or send them a letter including the name of the company, its address, the names of the people with whom you dealt, the dates and the details of the incident.

SACRAMENTO:
1719 24th Street
Sacramento, CA 95816
[916] 445-5741

FRESNO:
Room 3084
2550 Mariposa Street
Fresno, CA 93721
[209] 445-5009

SAN FRANCISCO:
185 Berry
San Francisco, CA 94107
[415] 557-3953

LOS ANGELES:
Room 8107
107 S. Broadway
Los Angeles, CA 90012
[213] 620-2652

SAN DIEGO:
Room 5008
1350 Front St.
San Diego, CA 92101
[714] 236-7345

C. RECOVERY FUND

California also provides a "Recovery Fund" which will reimburse a person for money he has lost as a result of some fraudulent act by a licensed real estate broker. However, you must first get a judgment against the broker and be unable to collect on the judgment. Contact the Department of Real Estate or an attorney for assistance.

125

CHAPTER 13

ORDERS OF EXAMINATION

What if your judgment creditor doesn't know what possessions you have, or where you work, or if you have a bank account? How is he to attach your assets? Or what if he knows where you work and attaches your wages, but you file a claim of exemption and win. Which one of your possessions would be the most valuable for him to go after next?

Well, a judgment creditor has various schemes of finding these things out. Through a procedure called an Order of Examination, he can ask you directly and you must respond.

A. HOW AN ORDER OF EXAMINATION WORKS

Under the law, the judgment creditor can go to the court and ask the judge to issue an Order of Examination requiring you to appear before the judge to answer, under oath, questions from the judgment creditor or his lawyer about your assets. If you receive such an order, you had better appear. If you do not, you can be held in contempt of court and face arrest. The only restriction on the judgment creditor is that he cannot require you to appear more often than once every 4 months.

B. RECEIVED AN ORDER BUT CANNOT APPEAR?

If you receive an Order of Examination but cannot afford to take time off from work or for some other reason cannot appear, call the judgment creditor or his attorney and explain your situation. Express to him your willingness to answer his questions over the phone or perhaps in person at another time. Since all the judgment creditor really wants is the information, in most instances he will be satisfied to get it over the phone if he feels that you are being cooperative and honest.

If you come to an agreement with a judgment creditor to answer his questions on the phone or at another time, ask him to send you a note verifying that you need not appear at the hearing date set in the order of examination. It is also wise to send him a note, with a copy to the court with the court number written on the top, and keep a copy of it for yourself. Here is an example.

NOTE—Never take any money with you to an Order of Examination. The creditor can ask you to empty your pockets or purse and can take any money in your possession.

181 Cottage Avenue
Yreka, California
May 17, 19____

Court No.   [*this number appears on
the order served on you*]

Mervyn Loya
610 Eugene Street
Redding, California

Dear Mr. Loya,

I am writing to confirm our phone conversation of May 15, 19___.

On that day, I answered all the questions you asked me on the
state of my assets and employment. You were satisfied with my
cooperation and stated that I need not appear in court on May 25, 19 __to
answer to the Order of Examination you had issued to me.

Very truly yours,

Julie Buttress

CHAPTER 14

CREDIT CARDS

A. AN AMERICAN FOLK TALE

In the early 1960's, Bank of America issued thousands of Bank Americards to people in Northern California. Seemingly if you had a charge account, a savings account, or a checking account, you received a card. A few months later, collection agencies were called in to repossess the cards of and collect on the many non-paying accounts.

Sounds like the old B. of A. took a beating, doesn't it? But you know better than that. Bank of America wouldn't be the largest bank in the country if they didn't know exactly what they were doing. As one representative of the bank told a friend, it was cheaper for them to just mail out the cards and take the loss on the bad debts than to send out applications, check credit reports on each person, and process all the forms.

Doing it their way, they accomplished their purpose in weeding out the bad accounts at less cost. In addition, they succeeded in fulfilling the goal of every credit card company whether a bank, oil company, department store or airline, namely: to get everyone to carry their particular brand of credit card; for credit cards are there to be used. The fact that lots of people got hopelessly in debt using credit cards that they never asked for and did not fully understand was just one of those unavoidable costs of doing business.

Credit cards are nothing other than very expensive loans. The interest rates on money not paid back within a given time period (usually 30 days) is around 18% a year.* The companies profit on the fact that most people do not pay off their credit card debt within that given time period. If they did, the companies would soon go out of existence. In effect, credit card companies want you to stay in debt, and some have begun charging people extra for paying their bills on time.

B. RECEIVING UNREQUESTED CARDS

The law has changed and now no card can be legally issued except in response to a request or application. If a company sends you a new unrequested card, it must take full responsibility for its use (Civ. Code Section 1747.05 and 15 U.S.C. Section 1642).

C. STOLEN OR LOST CREDIT CARDS

State law limits any loss you would incur if your card were lost or stolen. If you notify the company or bank which issued the card within a reasonable time after you discovered (or should have discovered) the loss or theft, you are not liable for any unauthorized use of your card. In no case can you be liable for more than $50 (Civ. Code Section 1747.20).

You can notify the credit card company by telephone, telegram, letter or postcard. If you decide to send a letter, keep a copy for your records. On the next page is a sample letter you can use. To find the address of the company, just look on the

---

*Not all states allow credit card companies to charge the outrageous interest of 18% a year. For example, New Jersey limits it to 15% and Connecticut to 12%.

postage-paid, addressed envelope or postcard they were required to send you with your card. If you have lost the envelope, look at any of the statements you have received from them in previous months, or look in your nearest metropolitan phone book. (Remember, a phone call is just as good as a letter, and most credit card companies have toll-free 800 numbers. You can call many of the major bank credit card offices 24 hours a day, seven days a week.)

D. IF YOU HAVE A PROBLEM WITH GOODS OR SERVICES BOUGHT WITH A CREDIT CARD

If you buy something, either goods or services, with your credit card and the item turns out to be defective you may refuse to pay for it if the seller refuses to replace or repair or otherwise correct the problem. Just notify the credit card company why you are withholding payment (15 U.S.C. Section 1666i. Civ. Code Section 1747.90).

There are no limitations on this right if the seller is owned or operated by the creditor-credit card company, as would be the case with a department store card, a gas company card, or an airline card, or if the creditor mailed you an advertisement for the item.

However, if it is a third party or bank credit card, such as BankAmericard, Mastercharge, American Express, your purchase must have been more than $50 and been made within your state or within 100 miles of your home.

2147 Porky Street
Davis, California
February 27, 19___

Shortage Oil Company
Credit Card Department
1 Main Street
Potato, California

Dear Sir:

    This is to inform you that I lost my Shortage Oil Company credit card yesterday, February 26, 19___ somewhere in the vicinity of Rose and Milvia Streets in Davis.

    I understand that under the law this letter serves as reasonably timely notice to you and that I am not liable for any unauthorized use of this card.

                                 Sincerely,

                                 Michael Pitre

132

E. IF THERE IS A BILLING ERROR

If you feel there is an error in your statement, your rights to satisfaction have greatly improved. 15 U.S.C. 1666. No more need you be frustrated by computers ignoring your complaint.

Begin by writing on a separate sheet of paper (not on the bill) 1) your name and account number, 2) an explanation of the believed error, and 3) the dollar amount of the believed error. Send it to the address given by the company for inquiries. Don't include your copy of the sales slip or other document unless you have a duplicate. The creditor must receive your notice within 60 days after the bill was mailed to you. See the sample letter below.

Now the burden falls on the credit card company. They must acknowledge receipt of your letter within 30 days unless they correct the billing within that time. Within 90 days after receiving your complaint, the company must either correct the mistake or explain why they believe the bill to be accurate.

IMPORTANT—If the credit card company does not comply with the 30- and 90-day requirements or with any of the other rules mentioned here, you may keep the disputed amount up to $50, whether or not an error had been made.

During the 90 days, or until the company comes up with an explanation, they cannot threaten or take any collection action against you for the disputed amount, though periodic statements may be sent to you. Nor can the amount be reported to a credit bureau or to other creditors as being delinquent.

If the creditor's explanation isn't satisfactory, you may notify them in writing within 10 days that you still refuse to pay. If they then report your delinquency to credit bureaus or other creditors they must also tell them that you do not believe you owe the money. They must also let you know to whom the reports were made. Once the matter is resolved, the company must notify the credit bureau and other creditors of the resolution. (See Chapter 4 on Credit Bureaus if you don't know how these outfits work.)

Under the law, if your complaint has not been worked out, whether it was a billing error or on account of a defective item (part D above) you can sue the creditor for $100 plus attorneys' fees. If the creditor is local this suit could be brought in Small Claims Court.

211 Judge Dee Drive
Fairfax, California
August 20, 19___

Big State Bank
1 State Plaza
San Anselmo, California

Dear People:

I wish to advise you of an error I believe you made in my Mastercharge statement.

My name is Robert Van Gulik, my account number is X201KJ. On March 25, 19__, I purchased with my Mastercharge two roundtrip tickets on Blue Airlines to Spokane, Washington, for $300. I lost the tickets a few days later and phoned the airlines for a duplicate set.

The charge for the first set of tickets appeared last month in my statement from you. My billing statement this month includes the charge for the second, duplicate set of tickets. Since I only used one set of the tickets I should not be charged for both of them.

I understand that under the law, you must acknowledge receipt of this letter within 30 days unless you correct this billing error before then, and that within 90 days you must correct the error or explain why you believe the amounts to be correct.

Sincerely,

Robert Van Gulik

F. OVERCHARGING YOUR LIMIT

Many credit cards have a dollar limit on your spending. For example, if your limit is $500 and you've used it up, you are not supposed to go out and make any further purchases.

Each merchant also has a limit. But his works the other way. He must call the credit card company for approval on purchases larger than a certain dollar amount. This amount, known as a "floor limit" differs with different kinds of merchants. If a customer purchases something for a dollar amount beneath that limit, the merchant will be reimbursed by the bank even if the customer fails to pay. If the purchase is above that limit and the debtor doesn't pay, the merchant will be reimbursed only if he first checks with the central office to okay the purchase.

When you go over your limit, the credit card company may get uptight. It depends upon whether you have been making payments regularly or not. Remember, they want you to use their card so they can get the interest. Unless you begin missing payments, they will probably leave you alone. Of course, if you miss payments, they will call or write and ask that you not use your card until you bring the balance below your limit.

CHAPTER 15

STUDENT LOANS

Student loans are basically the same as any other kind of loan. But since many people think of them as a special case, we include a separate chapter on student loans. Read chapter 7 on collection agencies before you go on. The college, the bank, or government will act pretty much the same as any other creditor or collection agency when it comes to collecting their money.

A. BANK LOANS

The government sponsors a federally insured student loan program in which the bank lends the money, but the government guarantees its payment. It is called the Guaranteed Student Loan Program and works like this:

    The bank lends you the money. You have no obligation to pay it back until 6 months after graduation or after you withdraw from school.* The federal government allows you to be a ½ time student and still maintain your student status. But many banks require you to follow a full time course program to

---

* Loans made before 1981 have a 9-month grace period.

keep your student status. Check with your bank to see whether ½ time is sufficient.

During the 6-month grace period, you are sent a notice to make contact with the bank to arrange a repayment schedule. If you do not answer their letters the bank will try other ways to contact you. But, essentially, the bank does not really care much whether you repay the loan or not. The reason for this mellowness is that if after 3 to 4 months you still haven't made any payments, the bank just turns the debt over to the federal Department of Education and asks for its money. They haven't lost anything except future interest. And at 9%, that isn't very much.* They can do much better using the money for other loans that pay higher interest.

For a number of years, the federal Department of Education depended on nearly 1000 full-time bill collectors to pursue people who defaulted on their student loans. They were pretty successful, returning more than $3 for every $1 it cost the taxpayers. More than 2000 federal lawsuits were filed against student defaulters in California alone.

But all this has changed. Now nearly all of these positions have been eliminated, and the collection of the loans is being contracted out to private bill collectors. The reasoning appears to be that the federal government should not be performing those functions which the private sector can handle. It will be interesting to see whether private collectors are as successful, since they will not have the clout of filing federal lawsuits against people in default, as the government did.

B. COLLEGE LOANS

Most college loans are National Direct Student Loans (NDSL). There are also some student loans from private or university sources.

The colleges generally work as follows:

For most loans there is a 6-month grace period after graduation or withdrawal. A letter to work out a repayment schedule is

---

* Loans made before 1981 have a 7% interest rate.

sent out during this period. If, after the nine months pass, no payment plan is set up, there is an additional waiting period of three to six months. The length of time depends upon the contacts they have with you, how in need the college is of the money, and how good your excuses are.

After this period passes and the college feels frustrated with your account, it will do one of the following:

1. turn the loan over to the school's general counsel's office for possible litigation

2. ask the state franchise tax board to withhold your tax return

3. contract with an outside collection agency to handle it*

4. request that the federal government get involved in the collection (assuming it's a federal loan). The federal government may either assist the college, or the college could return it to the government and let them worry about it.

C. WHAT TO DO

Generally, the way to deal with these bank or college loans is pretty much the same as the handling of any other debts. See chapter 7 on collection agencies. But here are a few things to consider.

Your bargaining power with banks will probably be more limited than with colleges. Bank loans require a $30 a month minimum repayment plan. If you cannot afford that amount, you might try to work something else out, but probably it won't work. The bank would just as well turn the loan over to the government, collect all their money and not worry about it. However, once the government holds the loan agreement, you probably would be able to work out a more convenient pay schedule. The government, having nowhere else to turn, would, as would any other bill collector, be pleased to receive some payments and not have to go through the hassle of filing a law suit and trying to collect on the judgment.

---

* The American National Educational Corp. in Chicago handles student loan default accounts for over 450 colleges in the country, including the University of California.

With loans from colleges you usually have much more flexibility than with banks. Though they too will often say they require a $30 minimum repayment, if they do not get it there isn't much they can do (though some will hold back diplomas or transcripts until payments are made). And colleges aren't going to contract out to a collection agency if they can avoid it. After all, you are an alumnus. So explain your situation and offer them what you can afford. Most likely they will be pleased that you are honestly trying to cooperate.

Here is a sample letter of the type you might send to your college to work out a repayment schedule.

```
                                        612 Pumpkin Road
                                        Riverside, California
                                        March 1, 19__

Donald Juneau
Student Loan Department
Arthur Rackham University
Alexandria Street
Big Sur, California

Dear Mr. Juneau:

    I was graduated from Arthur Rackham University in June, 19__.
While at the school, I borrowed $3,000 in National Direct Student
Loans.  I realize that my 6-month grace period is nearly over and that
I must begin making payments soon.

    In your letter of February 3, you said that I must repay a minimum
of $30 per month.  However, I have recently taken a job as a fortune
teller for Hometown Mystics and my income barely covers my expenses.
Nevertheless, I realize my obligations to repay and I do not want to back
out from these obligations.

    Consequently, I wish to make payments of $15 a month at this time.
Should I get a raise later on, I will try to increase my payments.

                            Very truly yours,


                            Christopher Michael Campbell
```

D. FILING BANKRUPTCY

You must now wait five years from the time the loan is first due (usually nine months after you leave school) before you can discharge it in bankruptcy. The only exception is if you can prove that it would be "undue hardship" to you or your family if the loan is not included in your bankruptcy petition.* There is no clear definition of what exactly qualifies as undue hardship. You might want to speak to a lawyer if you are thinking of filing under this provision. [11 U.S.C. Sec. 523(a)(8).] In some California cities, using the wage earner plan (Chapter 13) you may be able, in effect, to get rid of your loan without having to wait five years. It depends on how much the bankruptcy court in your area decides you need to pay to show "good faith" in trying to deal with your debts. (See Chapter 18, Section N.)

NOTE—Many student loans require co-signers. If the original debtor (the student) goes bankrupt, the lender can still go after the co-signer. This can also be done if the debtor simply refuses to pay. (See Chapter 1 on co-signers).

E. FEDERAL GOVERNMENT REPRISALS

The government has become defensive and will try to apply sanctions if you default on their loans. Some agencies say that they will deny you federal assistance later on because of your "bad record." We have heard, for example, that the Housing and Urban Development Office says that they may not approve certain guaranteed housing loans if you have not repaid your school debts. It is even possible that filing bankruptcy on the loan can cause problems on future government loan applications. It's something to think about, but probably need not be taken too seriously as the Federal Government is so big, cumbersome and clumsy that one department rarely knows what another is doing.

---

*Because of a legislative oversight, the requirement that student loans can't be discharged in bankruptcy until five years has gone by, or unless there is "undue hardship," has lapsed until October 1979, when it again is in force. Apparently student loans can be discharged in bankruptcy like any other debt prior to October 1979 (see Chapter 18).

F. STATUTE OF LIMITATIONS

The statute of limitations on student loans is six years. But the question is, from when do you start counting? Until recently, most attorneys assumed you began counting from the date on which you stopped making payments. If you had never made any payments, the time would have begun when the loan became due. (Student loans usually become due six or nine months after you leave school—not when you first obtained the loan.)

But a 1979 federal court decision in Pennsylvania* held that the six-year statute of limitations does not begin to run against the government (which guarantees payment of the loan) until the government pays off the lender. Since the government may wait a year or longer before it does this, the time in which you are still required by law to repay the loan can be substantially longer than six years.

Though federal courts in California are not bound to follow this Pennsylvania decision, they may. You should check with an attorney, do research on your own, or look at a later edition of this book to see whether there are any other cases which interpret the law differently.

* *United States v. Wilson,* 478 F. Supp. 488 (M.D.PA.1979).

CHAPTER 16

INCOME TAXES

In a world filled with more and more bureaucrats shuffling more and more pieces of paper saying less and less, there is a tax on everything except the air we breathe. If the air wasn't so filthy there would probably be a tax on it too. We don't have the ten lifetimes and hundred thousand or so pages necessary to discuss all the problems you can meet by failing to pay all these taxes. Here, we limit ourselves to failure to pay state and federal income taxes.

A. FAILURE TO PAY INCOME TAXES

If you file your tax return, but fail to pay all the money owed, you will get a notice telling you to pay up pronto. It's a good idea to do this, if possible. Should you fail to, you will get more notices (usually 3 or 4 in all). The final notice will tell you to pay up immediately or have your wages or property taken. Immediately means 10 days. The final notice will arrive approximately 3 months after the first notice from the federal tax people and 6 months after the first notice from the state. You can slow down this process by responding in writing to each notice. The notices are sent by a computer. When you respond, someone must get your file and deal with the response. This takes time, sometimes a lot of time. It makes little difference what you say in your letters as long as you don't make any false statements. One good approach is to simply ask for more time to pay and tell the government how hard your life is.

IMPORTANT—If you have been late on your tax payments in the past or have previously failed to pay taxes, you are probably labeled as a "Habitual Delinquent." If this happens, all pretence of politeness is dropped and you will receive only one notice to pay in 10 days or face wage attachments or the loss of other property.

B. FAILURE TO FILE A TAX RETURN

If you have paid taxes in the past and suddenly fail to file a return, you will probably be contacted. Should it be determined that you owe money, you will receive a series of notices as explained in section A above.

C. TAX AUDITS

If after a tax audit the government claims you owe more in taxes than you paid, you have the right to several appeals to higher level tax review boards and eventually to Tax Court. As long as you follow up your appeals, which may take several years, no one will get heavy. However, if you fail to appeal in the time allowed, you will receive a series of notices to pay up as outlined in section A and will face wage attachments and loss of

143

property if you don't. Audits are very tricky. See an attorney or tax accountant before getting involved in one.

D. TAX COLLECTIONS

The federal tax collector does not have to go to court to get a judgment against you before taking your wages and property. None of the exemptions discussed in chapters 10, 11, and 12 work against federal tax claims.

The State of California tax collector similarly does not have to spend time suing you and getting a judgment. However, the state has decided to recognize a debtor's right to the exemptions discussed earlier. If you owe state tax and the government goes after your wages, personal property or dwelling house, you may file for a claim of exemption to protect the item just as you would if a regular creditor were trying to attach it. If the state goes after your wages without a court hearing, it can take up to 25% of your net earnings. If this happens, you may request an administrative hearing to reconsider or modify the amount to be withheld. If the state files an application in court to attach your wages, it can take a much larger portion - up to 50%. The amount will depend upon what portion of your earnings you can prove is necessary for the support of yourself and/or your family.

Wage earners who have little in the way of valuable belongings can usually work out some form of monthly payments to catch up on unpaid taxes to the federal government, but the payments will be quite high. They don't have to make this sort of arrangement, but they often will because if they take your whole pay check you are likely to quit your job in disgust.

144

CHAPTER 17

CHILD SUPPORT AND SPOUSAL SUPPORT (ALIMONY)

Someplace over the dream rainbow of a man, a woman and their children living a happy, loving, harmonious life in which fulfillment is either complete, or just around the next split level ranch house, lies reality. Marriage just isn't working for lots of people—hundreds of thousands are involved in divorce proceedings every year. Divorce creates lots of money problems for lots of people, especially children. They like to eat, live in comfortable places and have an occasional lollipop. Divorce often puts these things in jeopardy. For those with low or moderate incomes, there is simply not enough money to support two households. An impossible situation is created in which something has to give.

A. CHILD SUPPORT AS PART OF A DIVORCE CASE

As part of a divorce proceeding, there is always an order for child support if there are children younger than 18. Either party can be ordered to support the children, but even though sex roles are changing rapidly, it is still usually the man. It is wise to pay child support on time and in full.*

If the parent ordered to support willfully fails to do so, he is in what is known as "contempt of court." Translated, this means big trouble. After a court hearing, he can be sent to county jail for contempt. In legal jargon the "contempt citation" process is called an "Order to Show Cause." This is an order to show up in court at a certain date and time to explain why you have not paid. A person receiving an "Order to Show Cause" concerning contempt better show up and better have a good story. Those who fail to attend will quickly be picked up on a warrant, tossed in jail for a day or two and escorted in to see the judge in handcuffs. Those who show up voluntarily but don't have a good story may enter the courthouse by the front door, but will certainly leave in a paddy wagon for a few days of free education behind county walls.

Of course, in addition to the criminal and civil contempt procedures outlined in this chapter, child support can be collected by all the normal methods of collecting judgments— wage, bank account, and personal property attachments, etc.

Wages can be assigned up to 50% for child support debts. The procedure goes as follows: If the parent who is responsible for child support payments (let's call the parent "Father") fails to make one month's payment within a 24-month period, the parent to whom support has been ordered (the "Mother") can sign an affidavit and petition the court to assign the wages of the father to satisfy the child support payment(s). However, the mother must first notify the father 15 days before she files this petition that she intends to seek this court relief of wage assignment. The court issues, without notice to the father, an order of assignment of wages to satisfy the court-ordered support. There is a 10-day period after the father's employer has been served before he must deliver to the father a copy of the assignment order.

If the father contends that his failure to pay did not occur

---

* Child support and custody as well as community and separate property and other legal rules affecting the marriage are discussed in **The People's Guide to California Marriage Law,** Warner and Ihara, Nolo Press, (see back of this book).

within the last 24 months or that he owes nothing, he can move to "quash" the assignment order, but he must do so within 10 days after service by his employer. In the meantime, the father's employer must continue to withhold and forward support as ordered by the court until he is notified that the court has granted the father's motion. The law also specifically provides that no employer shall use any assignment of wages as grounds for dismissal of the father. (Civil Code Section 4701.)

An order assigning salary or wages takes precedence over any assignment to other creditors. The court will order the employer to withhold and assign the regular child support payments of a certain sum per month until the arrearage is paid off. Combined, these amounts cannot exceed 50% of the father's income.

If the district attorney is involved in collecting this support from you, he may agree to accept less money. Therefore it is important that you pay attention to any court summons and show up at a hearing.

IMPORTANT—The existence of many other debts is absolutely no excuse not to pay child support. Similarly, the fact that a person spends money to support someone else's kids is not legal excuse not to support his own. There are tens of thousands of Californians who each year fail to take their support obligations seriously. It is one reason why county jails are so crowded.

1. Changing Child Support Amount

If a couple can agree to a child support amount as part of a compatible divorce, fine. If they can't and the matter goes into court contested, it is wise to have an attorney (see chapter 3). Child support is always changeable as circumstances change. Either party can petition the court to either raise or lower the amount at any time. It is also possible to change the amount by

AGREEMENT

John Amaro of 100 South Street, El Monte, California, and Sally Burton of 57 San Pablo Avenue, Redding, California, make the following agreement as regards the support of their two minor children, Anne Amaro and Roger Amaro.

1. That because John Amaro has suffered a serious illness which has reduced his income by 50% it is agreed that the $250 per month child support ordered in the divorce action between the parties is too high.

2. In order to avoid an expensive court proceeding to lower child support, and because John Amaro's health problems should improve in the next six months, it is agreed that John Amaro will pay to Sally Burton the sum of $125 per month for the support of Anne and Roger Amaro commencing May 1, 19   and terminating with the payment of November 1, 19   and that all additional amounts of support for this time period are forever given up by Sally Burton.

3. It is further agreed that the full amount of support ordered as part of the divorce proceedings ($250) will be paid commencing December 1, 19

_____	_____
Date	John Amaro
_____	_____
Date	Sally Burton

agreement without going to court. It would be wise to see a lawyer to get this sort of agreement drawn up, but at the very least write it down and sign it. Failure to do this means that unpaid support accumulates and becomes a debt that must be paid in the future.*

---

* See *After the Divorce*, Matthews, Nolo Press, for information, forms, and sample agreements for modifying child support.

IMPORTANT—Child support obligations are not dischargeable in bankruptcy. Also, certain attorney fees of the person receiving child support can't be wiped out in bankruptcy. This is a tricky area of the law and it is wise to consult a lawyer.

B. FAILURE TO SUPPORT YOUR CHILD IS A CRIME

The California legislature has done everything in its power to insure that children are supported. Penal Code section 270 states that the willful failure of a parent to support his or her children is a crime punishable by a fine of up to $1,000 and a jail sentence of up to one year, or both. It makes no difference whether the child's parents were married, or whether or not there has been a divorce proceeding.* If a father is disabled and has no income or savings, failure to support is not a crime. If he is unemployed he will not be prosecuted as long as he can show he is diligently seeking work. A court, in determining the ability of a father to support, will consider all of his income, including social insurance and gifts. If a father dies, or is otherwise unable to support, the duty falls on the mother.

When county authorities learn that a father is not supporting, they assign an employee of the District Attorney's Office, Family Support Division, to the case in situations where the mother is on welfare or may be forced to apply for welfare if support is not received.** Where welfare benefits are involved a social worker will alert the District Attorney automatically. The D.A.'s office first requests that the non-supporting father come in for a conference. It is an excellent idea to attend this sort of conference. Those who fail to do so are next contacted by a policeman with an arrest warrant. The purpose of the conference is to establish how much the father earns, whether or not he has other children to support, and to arrange for him to start making support payments. Be prepared to be shocked by how much the court wants. Children are expensive, and the Family Support Division normally tries to collect as much as the traffic will bear. By arguing, pointing out other obligations and the necessity of

---

* The rights and obligations of unmarried couples are discussed in detail in **The Living Together Kit,** Ihara and Warner, Nolo Press, (see back of this book).

** If the father can't be located the county can get access to federal social security information to find him. Once found, prosecution is simply transferred to the county where the father resides.

going to the grocery store now and again, a father can often get the county to agree to payments slightly less than those first proposed.

Once an amount has been agreed upon, it is important to make payments promptly and in full unless there is a good reason, such as illness or loss of work, to do otherwise. If there is such a reason it is important that the Family Support Division be told immediately what the problems are.

IMPORTANT—A divorce order, if there is one, takes priority over any agreement made with the District Attorney's Office. This means that county authorities will not bother a person who is in compliance with the child support provisions of a divorce order. It also means, however, that if a divorce order is entered setting child support at an amount higher than requested by the District Attorney, you must pay this higher amount.* It is perfectly possible to be hauled into court for civil contempt for failing to pay the full child support amount set out in a divorce order (see part A of this chapter), even though you are diligently paying a lower amount requested by the District Attorney.

We include here a guide for making child support orders used by the judges in Marin County. This will give you some idea as to whether you are paying too much or too little child support. **CAUTION:** This is a very general guide and should not be applied without consideration of all other relevant factors. Many judges use their own common sense in making child support awards and don't follow this type of chart at all.

C. SPOUSAL SUPPORT [ALIMONY]

A generation or two ago one tended to find women barefoot, pregnant and in the kitchen. No more. These days women are so busy getting themselves together that it's often hard to find

---

* If a parent falls one month behind in paying child support and the matter is brought to court, a judge will automatically order that his or her wages be assigned. (Civil Code Section 4701.)

SCHEDULE FOR CHILD SUPPORT PAYMENTS WHERE NO SPOUSAL SUPPORT IS ORDERED

Non-custodial Parent's NET Monthly Income*	One Child	Two Children	Three or More Children
$ 400.00	$ 100.00	$ 100.00	$ 100.00
500.00	125.00	150.00	175.00
600.00	150.00	200.00	225.00
700.00	150.00	250.00	275.00
800.00	150.00	250.00	300.00
900.00	175.00	275.00	350.00
1000.00	175.00	300.00	375.00
1200.00	200.00	350.00	450.00
1400.00	250.00	400.00	525.00
1600.00	250.00	450.00	600.00
1800.00	275.00	500.00	675.00
2000.00	300.00	550.00	750.00
Above 2000.00	Court's discretion		

NOTES

his schedule is prepared with the assumption that the custodial parent's et earnings are at least 25% less than that of the non-custodial parent, and hat there is no award of spousal support.

he rule for support is intended to be the same whether the custodial parent s the father or the mother.

f the non-custodial parent carries hospital, medical or dental insurance overing the children, the cost attributable to the children's coverage may e deducted from the support payments.

Income after compulsory deductions such as income tax, FICA, SDI and ompulsory retirement.

them at all. If they are in the kitchen it's only to see how the old man is doing with the spaghetti. An exaggeration? Perhaps, but times are changing fast and the old stereotype of papa at the office and mama at home is long gone. And it's about time, too.*

Spousal support (alimony), a necessary fact of life a generation ago, is for the most part outdated today. The woman who 20 years ago gave up school and other opportunities to devote herself to husband and children often needed support when the marriage went sour. Many times she was educationally and psychologically unable to support herself. Today this is far less true, but spousal support still exists.

Spousal support, in theory, can be awarded to either men or women. In fact it is almost always given to women. Judges, being old, and often from upper middle class backgrounds, still tend to think the world is like it was when they were in law school and all people of their social class received spousal support. A 65 year old judge has a lot of trouble relating to the life realities of people 30 or 40 years younger (mostly the people who get divorces). The result is that judges grant spousal support more often than is necessary.

The subject of spousal support comes up automatically as part of a divorce. Most younger women don't want it, desiring child support if they have children, but not wanting support for themselves. Older women want, and need, spousal support more often. Of course, a housewife of fifty who has raised a family and helped her husband become financially successful is entitled to a generous support award.

Failure to pay spousal support is not a crime. However, one can be found in contempt of court for willfully failing to pay spousal support if one has the ability to do so. As we said above, when discussing child support, a person can be sent to county jail for this sort of "contempt." A person's wages, bank account, or personal property can be attached, of course, if spousal support is not paid.

If no spousal support is awarded as part of a divorce proceeding, it can't be awarded later. However, if it is awarded, it can be changed later, unless the court specifically orders an exact amount of money for a limited period of time ($100 per

* California's joint custody law encourages both parents to share the rights and responsibilities of child-rearing by establishing a presumption that joint custody is in the best interests of the child(ren) if the parents agree. (Civil Code Section 4600.)

month for 4 years). If, for example, the court order said, "$100 per month until death, remarriage or further order of court," the amount could be changed by the judge at any time upon the petition of either husband or wife. Of course, both parties would get a chance to present their arguments to the judge if a change were proposed. Spousal support automatically ends upon the remarriage of the person receiving it.

Spousal support is a tricky area of the law. If you have any questions, see an attorney (see chapter 3).

IMPORTANT—Spousal support obligations are not discharge-able in bankruptcy. Also, certain attorney fees of the person receiving spousal support can't be wiped out in bankruptcy. This a tricky area of the law and it is wise to consult a lawyer.

We include here guidelines used by judges in Marin County in awarding spousal support. Remember, these are only guidelines and should be changed to fit the facts of each individual situation.

GUIDE LINES FOR DURATION OF SPOUSAL SUPPORT
AFTER DISSOLUTION OR LEGAL SEPARATION

Length of Marriage	Duration of Support
Under 12 years	It is presumed that spousal support shall terminate after a period equivalent to one-half the duration of the marriage.
12 to 25 years	There is no presumption for termination of spousal support. The following factors to be considered [whether or not it shall terminate]: wife's education, training, work experience, health and age; husband's ability to pay support; wife's eligibility for social security.
Over 25 years	It is presumed that permanent spousal support shall not terminate unless wife remarries.

1. Presence or absence of preschool children to be considered if husband has income above minimum.

2. Special consideration to be given to the ill health of either spouse.

3. After 25 years of marriage, the wife is presumed to require spousal support.

4. Duration of temporary spousal support payments should be taken into account.

AMOUNT OF SPOUSAL SUPPORT

If the net earnings of one spouse are $300.00 to $600.00, maximum support to the other spouse is ⅓ of that income.

If the net earnings of one spouse are over $600.00, maximum support to the other spouse shall not exceed 40% of that amount.

If there is both spousal and child support, the combined order should not exceed 50% of the supporting spouse's net income.

No spousal support shall be provided to any spouse, who, following dissolution, has income sufficient to maintain his or her standard of living.

CHAPTER 18

BANKRUPTCY

Want to get rid of all your debts at one time? Your creditors have been harassing you and you are at your wits end trying to cope. Perhaps your wages have been garnished, or bill collectors have made it clear that a garnishment is just around the corner. As we have indicated throughout this book, you do have one ultimate weapon—bankruptcy. If, after reading this book carefully you realize that bankruptcy is the only sensible course of action, you or your lawyer can quickly wipe out the great majority of your debts by filing some simple papers.*

A. WHAT IS IT?

Bankruptcy was set up by the federal government to help you wipe out most, if not all of your debts. Your debts to the butcher, the baker, the candlestick maker, the doctor, the oil company, the finance company, the phone company, the furniture store can all be eliminated. Very few debts can not be wiped out and we'll talk about those later on.

You can file bankruptcy at any time. It doesn't matter whether you're working or not. The only restriction is that you

---

* The best source of further information on bankruptcy is Kosel, *Bankruptcy: Do It Yourself*, Nolo Press (see end of this book for more information).

must wait six years between filings. Bankruptcy is a relatively simple procedure involving filing some papers in federal court, paying a $60 filing fee, and paying attorney's fees of somewhere between $200 and $300.

If you have any "assets" of value ("assets" are anything you own, including money), the bankruptcy court may take some of these and use them to pay off your creditors. But the law has made a large exception here and permits you to keep part and often all of your possessions. You can usually keep an inexpensive car, your home, $1,000 in a savings and loan institution, $1500 in a credit union, your furniture, clothes, appliances, and tools or equipment you need in your trade or profession.* These assets are called "exempt" assets and are explained in section F below.

Bankruptcy is a powerful remedy. It's as if you took a blanket and laid it over all your debts, recited a few magic words and chants, removed the blanket and Poof—your debts are gone. But like any powerful remedy, it only works well if used with care and understanding. Just as you wouldn't undertake a major operation to remove a worry wart, you wouldn't file bankruptcy to zap a $25 debt.

B. WHY FEEL GUILTY?

"Low down payments," "easy credit," "36 months to pay," so goes the salesman's song. You are bombarded with special deals, sales and every kind of pitch to wear down your resistance and get you to buy and buy and then buy some more. The salesmen were always so friendly and kind. Then it happened. You missed a payment and suddenly their smiles disappeared. They forgot about all the sweet words they once sang to you. They wanted the money. And they wanted it immediately. Any way you came up with it was fine. But you had better come up with it pronto. Soon you got calls at all hours of the day. Letters threatening law suits arrived at your home. "Visitors" from collection agencies came by. Each time they succeeded in frightening you a bit more. They did their best to make you feel guilty.**

---

* This assumes you use the exemptions under California law rather than under federal law.

** There are several ways to stop this bill collection harassment quickly. (See Chapter Seven.)

This kind of scare-guilt pattern has been with us for a long time. But so has the concept of bankruptcy, partly as a counteraction to it. In fact, the idea of bankruptcy has been with us for nearly 175 years. Bankruptcy was designed to give people a new start in life at a time when debts were imprisoning them and weighing them down with unnecessary guilt. It exists to give the little guy a chance to get out of the clutches of large corporations. Back in 1800, Congress first experimented with a bankruptcy act. The first modern bankruptcy law was written in 1898 and revised in 1938. This law was entirely re-written in 1978 and took effect in October 1979. Bankruptcy is as American as apple pie and creditors know it.

Hundreds of those same corporations which enticed you into debt and scream the "horrors of bankruptcy" and other "terrifying" phrases at you use their own good business sense and file bankruptcy each year. So why should you feel any more guilty than they themselves?

C. ARE YOU GETTING DIVORCED?

Often people who are in the process of divorce think of filing bankruptcy. They would like to wipe their whole slate clean and begin again with their new individual lives. But in reality, the financial problems are probably still bound up with the emotional entanglements.

The emotional and financial worries should be kept separate. Remember, except for spousal or child support, you cannot go to jail for not paying your debts. (And even here you can only go to jail if you have the money but refuse to pay. See chapter 17.) So relax and work out your divorce settlement. Then give thought to your financial problems and figure out the best way to deal with them. You might decide that you need to file bankruptcy to get rid of most debts and be able to pay the important ones, child and spousal support. Whatever you conclude, at least you'll be on top of it.

D. DEBTS YOU CANNOT WIPE OUT IN BANKRUPTCY

There are certain debts which you must continue to pay even if you file bankruptcy. These are called "non-dischargeable" debts. ("Dischargeable" debts are all the debts you can get rid of in bankruptcy.) Here is a list of the non-dischargeable debts:
1. State and federal taxes
2. Fines (criminal cases, traffic violations, etc.)
3. Child support
4. Spousal support (alimony)
5. Some lawyers fees connected with a divorce settlement involving support (this is complicated—see an attorney)
6. Claims against you for a willful or malicious act you committed. A willful act is one where you intentionally injure someone or someone's property. They are uncommon. Most automobile accidents, for example, are not intentional but rather the result of negligence, and so are dischargeable in bankruptcy. However, drunk driving resulting in an injury might be considered a willful act.

7. A debt you obtained by fraud or false pretenses such as by using bad checks or lying on a credit application. A common example of a false financial statement could be where you did not list all the debts you had at the time you were borrowing the money and the creditor relied on the accuracy of your statement in determining whether to lend you the money. If you have any problems here, discuss them with a lawyer before you file.

8. Student loans due for less than five years (see Chapter Fifteen, Section D).

9. Items you purchased recently on credit will not be discharged if the judge determines that you had already decided to file for bankruptcy when you bought them. Judges feel that most people heavily in debt and ready to file for bankruptcy do not go out spending even more—unless they're trying to take advantage of their soon-to-be bankruptcy.

10. Debts you forgot to list on the forms, or which you left off for other reasons (such as thinking you don't really owe them or they'll never go after you for them), are not dischargeable.

E. SECURED DEBTS VS. UNSECURED DEBTS

Secured debts are those in which the creditor keeps legal title of the property until you pay off the debt. Unsecured debts are everything else. Most debts you have are probably unsecured (see chapter 5).

When you file bankruptcy, you wipe out all your unsecured debts with one fell swoop. Plus you get to keep any property you bought on that debt. With secured property, however, you usually must give back the merchandise to get rid of the debt.* If you want to keep the item, you must continue making payments on it.

---

* However, if you put up exempt household property, such as furniture, as collateral for a loan, and the loan was not made in order for you to purchase the property itself, you can discharge the loan and keep the property.

Here is a partial list of unsecured debts:
1. All credit card purchases
2. Utility bills
3. Medical bills
4. Loans from banks, credit unions, and finance companies where no collateral is required, only your signature
5. Union dues
6. Attorney fees

Secured debts would probably be:
1. Your car, if you're making payments on it
2. Your house, if you have a mortgage
3. Some furniture, depending on the purchase agreement

If you no longer own the property which is security on a debt, because it was lost or stolen or because of some other reason, you may still be responsible for it. If this is your problem, discuss it with your lawyer before you file.

F. EXEMPT ASSETS—YOU CAN KEEP MOST OF YOUR PROPERTY

When you file bankruptcy, you must list all your assets. Your assets are anything you own including your bank account, personal possessions, and wages. The bankruptcy court may be able to take some of these and use them to pay off your creditors. However, the law has long said that the bankrupt (that is, the person who files bankruptcy) should be able to keep most necessary things. The assets which you can keep are called "exempt" assets and usually include a great deal of what you own.

There are two distinct exemption systems—state and federal. You can choose either one; you cannot take what you think are the best parts of each. Generally, if you own a home you are probably better off with the California program, since its protection of homes is greater than the federal system. If you rent, the federal system is likely to be more attractive—it allows for greater flexibility. But only you can decide. Compare the two systems and see.

THE CALIFORNIA EXEMPTION SYSTEM

Under the California system, you can keep:

Your home (see Chapter 12 for amounts).

A mobile home, housetrailer, or houseboat, if you reside in it, up to a value of $30,000 for a single person under 65, and $45,000 for a family, providing you do not claim any other home as an exemption.

Inexpensive motor vehicle if your equity is $500 or less. If it is worth more than this amount, the court may take it from you, but it will have to give you up to $500 in cash.

Furniture, appliances, household furnishings

1 shotgun and 1 rifle

Clothes

TV, radio, piano

Tools, equipment, instruments, books used in your trade, business or profession up to a value of $2,500

$1,000 in a savings and loan company

$1,500 in a credit union

Life and health insurance policies

Retirement and pension benefits

Federal and state benefits like social security, welfare, and unemployment compensation.

Since these assets and some others are also exempt from attachment by creditors, they are discussed in chapter 10 on wages; chapter 11 on motor vehicles, savings, and other personal possessions; and chapter 12 on protecting your home and land. The discussion in these chapters is much more thorough and covers the extent of and the limitations on exempt assets. Read them if you wish to know this material in detail. **If you have any non-exempt assets, you can often convert them into exempt assets.** For some examples, see chapter 11, section C.

THE FEDERAL EXEMPTION SYSTEM*

Under this system you can keep:
- A residence (including a house, housetrailer, mobile home, condominium, houseboat) with an equity up to $7,500.
- A motor vehicle with an equity of $1,200.
- Any of the following, as long as your equity in each item is not worth more than $200 (if sold now—not what you paid for it).

  furniture
  appliances
  clothes
  household goods
  books
  animals
  crops
  musical instruments
- Jewelry up to a total equity value of $500
- Tools of your trade up to $750 equity
- Life insurance, health insurance, disability, retirement benefits, and government benefits such as welfare, unemployment insurance, veterans' benefits, social security.

You also get $400 in any property *plus* the unused amount in the first item above. Thus, if you do not own a home, housetrailer, etc., you can take this total of $7,900 ($7,500 + $400) to cover any other property you would like to exempt. These might include bank accounts, a second car, or an item which is too expensive to be covered by the exemptions above, e.g., a silver-plated flute valued at more than the $200 exemption for musical instruments.

This $7,900 allowance can give you greater flexibility than can the California system, providing you do not own a home.

EXAMPLE—Shirley owns a car worth $750, a harp worth $1,000, and a nine-year-old purebred cocker spaniel named Janice. She also has a checking account with a present balance of $150 and a savings account at a bank with a present balance of $200.

Under California law, none of her property is exempt. Unless Shirley sells all of her property (before she files for

---

* Section 11 U.S.C. Section 522(d).

bankruptcy) and closes her bank accounts and puts the money in a credit union, savings and loan, or some other exempt asset, she will lose all of it—except her dog, which, with all due respect to Janice, isn't worth enough for the trustee to bother with. But if Shirley picks the federal exemption system, she can keep all of her property without bothering about specific exemptions or property transfers because it is worth less than $7,500.

However, if Shirley owned a home, she might decide to use the California exemption system. It would protect up to $30,000 of equity in her home, while the federal exemption system would only protect $7,500 of equity.

G. WHAT ABOUT CO-SIGNERS?

If someone else like a friend or family member signed the loan agreement or contract along with you, then even though you can rid yourself of the debt by filing bankruptcy, unless your co-signer also files, he or she is still responsible for payments. If that other person is, or was, your spouse, you may want him or her to also file bankruptcy with you. Your spouse should probably file if:

1. He or she co-signed the debts,

2. The debts were for necessities such as rent, food, clothes, and medical bills, and you file for the California exemptions,

3. He or she will be coming into some money, whether by working, inheritance, or whatever. If any terms of the loan agreement or contract were changed during the time it was in effect and the co-signer did not sign to the new change, the co-signer may not be responsible for payments. Check with an attorney and see Chapter 1, Section D on co-signers.

H. IS NOW THE RIGHT TIME TO FILE BANKRUPTCY?

The best time to file bankruptcy is when:

1. You are actually going to lose something if you do not file;

2. You do not expect any debts to come up in the near future;

3. You will be able to balance your income and expenses after bankruptcy; and

4. You will actually wipe out debts totaling at least ⅓ of your yearly income, or ¼ if you have a low income.

The following sections will help you figure out when the time is right. Remember, you must wait 6 years before you can file again. So take the "bath" fully prepared, and walk away "clean."

Ask yourself the following:

1. Am I Really Going To Lose Something If I Don't File Now?

If you have a low income and you don't own very much, you may be "judgment proof." Judgment proof means that you have nothing which a creditor can take from you. Filing bankruptcy would be silly, of course, if the creditor can't get anything anyway.

However, if you expect to come into some money soon (other than welfare, social security, unemployment compensation, or other government benefits), perhaps by working or getting an inheritance, you may want to file now. If you don't, the money you receive may be attached by the creditors for payments. By filing bankruptcy, you'll protect yourself by getting rid of these debts for good.

2. Do I Expect Any Debts To Come Up In The Near Future?

If you expect to be owing more money in the near future, such as for hospital or medical bills, or because of an accident where you were at fault and didn't have insurance, be sure these are also included.

3. Will I Be Able To Balance My Income And Expenses After Bankruptcy?

People are often so anxious to file bankruptcy to solve all their problems that they never think of what their financial situation will be afterwards. Yet, if it is no better than before, you will have wasted your opportunity to file.

Give a little thought to your financial position after you wipe out your present debts. Will you soon be accumulating new debts or will you be able to keep your new financial position in harmony with the life style you want to live?

Take a look at the chart below. Fill it out and see where it leads you. If it leads you nowhere, bankruptcy may not do you much good.

FINANCIAL POSITION AFTER BANKRUPTCY

Monthly Expenses

Rent or Mortgage Payments and Utilities	_____
Food	_____
Medical Bills	_____
Clothes	_____
Property Taxes	_____
Alimony or Child Support	_____
Transportation	_____
Entertainment	_____
Other Expenses	_____
TOTAL	_____

Monthly Income

Employment	_____
Other Source of Income	_____
Food Stamps	_____
TOTAL	_____

Now look at these totals. Unless your monthly income total is greater than your expenses, you'll soon be in trouble again. If possible, wait until you get yourself financially together and have enough income to support yourself. Then file bankruptcy, get rid of your debts and have a bright future.

Of course, if your monthly income is greater than your monthly expenses, now may be the right time for you to file.

You have read through three items to consider before you file bankruptcy. Now here is one more and this is the **Big One.** So hold on.

4. Exactly How Much Will You Wipe Out In Bankruptcy?

Bankruptcy may not wipe out all your debts. Some may be "non-dischargeable." On others, you will have to give up the item that the creditor holds as security, if you want to cancel the debt. And then there are those loans from friends and relatives, which you'd like to still keep paying. So read through this section with us and see exactly how much of your debt you'll be actually wiping out.

a) Add up all your debts.

b) Subtract all those debts which are non-dischargeable (see section D above).

c) This amount is your working total.

d) Though you can wipe out your entire working total, you may not want to.

Example 1: If you have any secured debts and you want to keep the property the debt is secured on, you will have to continue making payments on it. For example, if you have a stereo set worth $1,000 and you only owe $200 on it, it would probably be worth keeping. (Read section E above about secured property.) Example 2: If you owe money to a friend or relative, you may want to continue paying him.

So consider which debts you really want to get rid of, and which you will still be paying off after bankruptcy. Subtract the debts you expect to still be paying after bankruptcy from your working total.

166

e) The total you arrive at should be at least ⅓ of your yearly take home pay. If you are a person who makes a low income, you may want to use the figure of ¼ of your yearly take home pay instead of ⅓. If the total is less, it probably is worth figuring out another way to beat the bill collector. Keep bankruptcy in reserve until you hit the big time.*

---

*Of course, there will always be exceptions and special cases to this general guideline. For example, if your wages are being attached and there is no other way to stop and you are afraid of losing your job, you may want to file bankruptcy, even if your total amount of debt is less than 1/3 or 1/4 of your yearly income.

EXAMPLE 1

Robert Benjamin of Eureka, California, has just gotten a divorce from his wife Karen. In the settlement he agreed to pay all the debts they contracted during their marriage. He also is required to pay her alimony and child support. He is unable to pay all his debts and several collection agencies are preparing to attach his wages. He has a take-home income of $22,000 per year.

These are his total debts:

Alimony (monthly payment for February)	$ 350
Child Support (monthly payment for February)	$ 350
Hospital Bills	$ 3,000
House	70,000
Mastercard	$ 500
1979 Maverick	$ 4,800
Visa	$ 1,000
Bedroom Set	$ 4,200
Aunt Mae	$ 400
TOTAL	$84,600

1. His total debt is $84,600.

167

2. Alimony and child support are "non-dischargeable" debts and so are subtracted from his total debts:

$84,600
−700
TOTAL $83,900

3. His working total is $83,900.

4. Now he decides which of his debts he will still be paying after bankruptcy. He want to keep the house ($70,000) and the car ($4,800), both of which are secured debts and both of which have a sale value in excess of the amount owed. He also wants to repay Aunt Mae ($400). These three debts total $75,200. Subtracting these debts from his working total:

$83,900
−75,200
he gets $ 8,700

5. If Robert files bankruptcy, he will actually wipe out $8,700. Since Robert is in bad financial shape and he owes more than ⅓ of his annual take home pay, he should consider bankruptcy, wipe out his less important debts, and concentrate on paying spousal and child support, mortgage, and car payments, and on just getting settled again.

Robert should consider one more thing. If his former wife Karen co-signed on any of the debts, she is also responsible for them. If he files bankruptcy, she may get stuck (see section G above). Robert should speak to a lawyer about this and see whether Karen should file with him.

EXAMPLE 2

Anita Parker of Redlands, California, has an income (take-home pay) of $10,500 per year.

These are her total debts:

Dentist Bills	$275
Shortage Oil Credit Card	$150
Big John's Department Store	$225
Back Taxes	$200
Traffic Tickets	$60
Piano	$300
Friend Kathy	$100
1973 Datsun	$400
Bank Credit Card	$350
TOTAL	$2,060

1. Her total debts are $2,060.

2. Traffic tickets and back taxes are "non-dischargeable" and so are subtracted from her total debt:

$$\begin{array}{r} \$2,060 \\ - 260 \\ \hline \text{TOTAL} \quad \$1,800 \end{array}$$

3. Her working total is $1,800.

4. Now she decides which of her debts she will still be paying after bankruptcy. She wants to keep the piano ($300) which is secured property. She also wants to repay friend Kathy ($100). These two debts total $400. Subtracting this amount from her working total:

$$\begin{array}{r} \$1,800 \\ - 400 \\ \hline \text{she gets} \quad \$1,400. \end{array}$$

5. If Anita files bankruptcy, she will actually wipe out $1,400. Since this is far less than ⅓ of her yearly take home pay, Anita would be better off waiting and not waste her power to file bankruptcy on such a relatively small amount. She should read through this book and see if she can come up with other ways to deal with her bills.

I. READY TO FILE?

1. See A Lawyer

There are simple bankruptices and more difficult ones. Generally, we feel that if you intend to file bankruptcy, you would be wise to hire a lawyer. A mistake like forgetting to include certain debts or not putting your assets in order before you file could be very costly. The fee you pay an attorney is probably worth the psychological security of knowing you will accomplish what you intended. (See our chapter on attorneys to help you pick one.) But if your bankruptcy is a relatively simple one, you may be able to do it yourself. For those people with simple bankruptcies or for the growing number who feel strongly that they want to handle their own affairs or who can't relate to lawyers, we suggest you get a copy of *Bankruptcy: Do-It-Yourself* by attorney Janice Kosel (available from Nolo Press; see back of this book). This book contains all the forms and instructions necessary to do your own bankruptcy. You may also wish to have an attorney review the filled-out forms for accuracy. S/he shouldn't charge you more than $50–$100 for this service.

2. How Does Bankruptcy Work?

We won't go into much detail on how the filing of bankruptcy actually works. Your lawyer will handle most of that. But generally, here's what happens.

You list all your debts and claims against you, your assets, and other general information in a petition which is filed with the federal court.

There is a $60 filing fee for each person who files, though it can often be paid in installments.

A few weeks later, a brief hearing with the trustee (the person who supervises your bankruptcy) and the creditors will be held to give them the opportunity to question you about any irregularities in your petition. You must attend this hearing. It is fairly informal and normally lasts less than 15 minutes. If either side claims that a serious and unresolvable problem exists, there may be a second hearing in the presence of a judge.

If you have any assets which are not exempt (see section

F), they will be turned over to the trustee and divided among your creditors.

The trustee can also recover from your creditors any extraordinary payments (normal monthly payments are O.K.) you made or possessions you gave to any of them within 90 days before you file bankruptcy. If the extraordinary transfer was to a relative, it can be questioned for up to a year. So during this period only make those payments which are essential (like your mortgage and car payments). **Don't pay off friends or relatives,** because they will probably just have it taken away, which is more painful than never getting it in the first place. Also, don't give any of your property away or sell it for less than it's worth.

A few months later, you must attend a court hearing. If all is in order, the bankruptcy judge will inform you that you have been given a final discharge of the debts you listed which are dischargeable.

J. REAFFIRMING YOUR DEBT

After you file bankruptcy, your creditors will soon be swooping down upon you to get you to agree to pay off the debt to them anyway, that is, to "reaffirm" the debt. They will use such tactics as making you feel guilty, telling you that your credit rating is now shot for life unless you agree to pay, and persuading you that you need that new vinyl sofa or piano or any other secured property which they can take back unless you agree to pay.

Be careful and make certain you don't agree to anything without careful thought. You are not required to keep anything or even to talk to the creditor. Remember, you filed bankruptcy in the first place to get rid of your debts. If you do wish to keep some item they can take away, bargain with them for it. **Never** offer more than what it is worth now, no matter how much you owed them for it before bankruptcy. For example, if you owed them $700 on a secured piano and it is worth only $300, offer them $300 or less, if you want to keep it. The creditor, even if he says otherwise, is glad to get anything from you and will probably accept your offer. But be careful. Don't let them trick you into signing a new contract which says that if you fail to make

171

payments, they can reinstate the full amount you owed before you filed bankruptcy.

NOTE—If you do reaffirm a debt, it must now be approved by the court, and you may change your mind within 30 days.

At the hearing, the judge will consider whether your reaffirming the debt is in your best interests—that is, the creditor didn't pressure you into doing it. The judge will also advise you of the effects of reaffirming the debt.

K. WHAT ABOUT YOUR CREDIT RATING?

If you are considering bankruptcy, your credit rating is probably not that good to begin with. Bankruptcy is not likely to hurt it much. However, since the Bankruptcy law changed and made it easier for people to file bankruptcy, there has been a substantial increase in the number of people who have declared bankruptcy. As a result, creditors are much less willing to lend to you if you have declared bankruptcy. Don't be entirely put off, especially if you have a job or some income and can explain the circumstances surrounding your decision to declare bankruptcy.

Some problems may arise if you intend to buy a house or wish to keep a good rating with your credit union. Before a lending institution will take a mortgage on your home, they will probably check to make sure you can keep up with the payments. Your credit union may also wish to discuss your financial situation carefully, if you intend to continue using its services. Banks also may give you some guff if you want a loan.

L. EMPLOYER PROBLEMS

It doesn't seem that likely, but if you think your employer might get uptight and fire you if you file bankruptcy, mention the possibility of your filing to him and see his reaction.

If you intend to take a job where you must be bonded, such as a guard or bank messenger, you may have trouble getting the bond. Contact the Human Resources Development Department under California in the white pages of the phone book. They may be able to help you.

M. STILL WORRIED?

If you are still worried about what might happen to you if you file bankruptcy, **relax.** So many people file bankruptcy each year that creditors have become accustomed to it. After all, bankruptcy is as much a part of the system as credit.

N. CHAPTER 13—PAYING OFF YOUR DEBTS

There is a program set up under federal bankruptcy law which helps certain debtors pay off their debts under the protection of the court, without any further dealings with creditors or collection agencies. It is called Chapter 13 of the Bankruptcy Act. The bankruptcy court takes a certain percentage of each paycheck and divides it among your creditors. (Consumer Credit Counselors informally try to do much the same thing for a much lower cost to you. See Chapter 3, section C.) The program usually lasts three years, though it may run up to five.

1. How Much Do You Have to Repay on Your Debts?

The law sets out no clear standard on what you have to pay under the program. As a result, bankruptcy courts have differed on the repayment plans they will accept from the debtor. There are basically four approaches:

1. Any amount. The court will accept any amount you agree to pay—even a plan to repay at the rate of 1% of your debts. The reasoning behind accepting this is that anything you agree to pay is better for the creditors than nothing—which is what they would likely receive in bankruptcy. This program is—as you would probably expect—the least common.

2. Must be at least 70%. Many courts require that you agree to pay off at least 70% of your debts. This percentage is used because the law says that if you pay off at a lesser percentage, your Chapter 13 program actually amounts to a discharge in bankruptcy. In that case you must wait six years to do it again. If you set up a repayment schedule over 70%, you can

file regular bankruptcy at any time, should the Chapter 13 program not work out.

3. Good faith plus 70%. Some courts require more than merely offering to repay 70% of your debts. They expect you to show "good faith"—that is, to show that the percentage you propose is the best you can do. Some courts interpret this to mean that anything less than a 100% repayment plan is not good faith.

4. Good faith alone. A few courts allow you to pay at any percentage—even less than 70%—as long as you show good faith. You must show that this is all you can afford—that your basic living expenses, such as shelter, food, clothing, utilities, transportation, medical, etc., leave you nothing more to help pay your debts.

Because the bankruptcy courts differ, it depends on where you live as much as on anything else what percentage repayment plan will be accepted. You probably should talk to a lawyer or to legal aid to find out what the situation is in your community—and whether the law has changed.

You may also wish to examine a copy of a new book on how to do your own Chapter 13 by Janice Kosel, available from Nolo Press by January 1982.

2. What Does It Do?

Here's what happens if you participate in the plan. It stops any unsecured creditor from:
1. filing suit against you
2. attaching your wages or other assets of yours
3. making any contact with you
4. speaking to your employer about your debts, or
5. going after co-signers who have signed notes with you.

It also completely stops all service charges, late charges, fines, collection charges, additional court costs, most interest charges, and additional charges.

Though it doesn't bind secured creditors, it does put pressure on them to agree to the plan.

3. Lawyer's Fee

The lawyer's fee is somewhere around $300, though you may be able to find one who will charge less (see chapter 3). However, under the plan, your lawyer is treated as any other unsecured creditor of yours, receiving part payment each month. You cannot pay him or her in advance, nor can you make direct payments to him or her later on.

4. You Can Still File Bankruptcy

Though Chapter 13 is written into the bankruptcy law, it is not the same as a regular bankruptcy. Therefore, if you agree to pay at least 70% of the amount of your debts, you can at any time (providing you haven't filed bankruptcy within the last 6 years) terminate the Chapter 13 and file a regular bankruptcy. You might want to do this, for example, if suddenly you got hit with some additional medical expenses or an automobile accident judgment or whatever else you cannot pay off under your Chapter 13. Of course, filing bankruptcy will mean paying a lawyer another $300 or so to do your bankruptcy.

On the other side of the coin, if you have filed bankruptcy within the last 6 years, and thus cannot file a regular bankruptcy, you can still go through a Chapter 13.

CHAPTER 19

FREQUENTLY ASKED QUESTIONS

In the several years since this book was first published we have participated in hundreds of lectures, classes and talk shows on radio and T.V. Many thousands of people have asked us many thousands of questions. Not remarkably, many of the same questions are asked again and again. At times we have almost felt as if somewhere there existed a Bureau of Wrong Information whose sole purpose was to confuse people.

Here are some of the questions:

Q. Is it true that if a collection agency accepts a payment from me after they have gotten a judgment on a particular debt, they can no longer attach my wages or other property?

A. No. See Chapters 8-12. If you owe money, the creditor is entitled to try and get it from you. If you are behind in your payments, he can take a payment (and often does) and still sue you, or if he has already sued you, still attach your wages, This may be nasty, but its not illegal. If you wish to exact a promise from a creditor that he won't do some particular thing in exchange for a payment, get it in writing.

Q. I am six months behind on paying for my car and they are trying to repossess it. Can I stop them by starting to make monthly payments?

A. Probably not. This is a variation of the first question. Almost all written contracts have an "acceleration clause". This means that if you miss a payment the whole amount of the debt comes due. Once this happens you can't reinstate the debt by making one payment or even making all the past due payments, unless the creditor agrees in writing to your plan.

Q. Can I file bankruptcy if I'm working?

A. Yes. In fact, the best time to file is when your financial situation will improve as a result. Obviously, this is true when you are working, since you can keep wages you earn after you file. See Chapter 18.

Q. What is the statute of limitations on student loans?

A. Six years. But computation of the time can vary considerably. It may depend on when the federal government paid off the bank on your loan. (See Chapter 15.)

Q. Am I entitled to a statement of reasons if the bank refuses to grant me a loan or offers me a loan at terms I don't like?

A. Yes, absolutely. See Chapter 4.

Q. What can I do if I buy something with a credit card and the item turns out to be defective?

A. In most instances, you can refuse to pay the credit card company if the seller refuses to repair or replace it. See Chapter 14.

Q. Can I file claims of exemption against tax collectors?

A. You can on state tax claims but not on federal claims. See Chapter 16.

Q. Should I check my credit bureau file even if I am not interested in getting credit right now?

A. Yes, Since credit bureaus are notorious in having misleading or even downright inaccurate information, it is good if you check it out now before it is given out to creditors or others. See Chapter 4.

Q. I am receiving spousal and child support under a written agreement. Can I apply for a bank loan or a credit card and use these support payments as my basis for "earnings"?

A. Yes. See Chapter 4.

Q. My creditor is threatening to attach my wages. Can he do it?

A. It depends. First he must file a lawsuit and get a judgment against you. That takes time. Then it depends on how much you are earning and whether you need all your earnings for the support of yourself or your family. See Chapters 8, 9 and 10.

Q. How much should I be in debt before I file bankruptcy?

A. It depends on many factors such as: to whom you owe the money, what assets you have which aren't exempt, whether you expect other debts to come up soon, and whether you are working or have another source of income. See Chapter 18.

Q. Can I file bankruptcy to wipe out student loans?

A. Yes, only if you wait five years from the date that the loan is due, unless you can prove hardship (see Chapter 15). But you can file under Chapter 13 of the bankruptcy act, and this may be almost as good. (See Chapter 15.)

Q. Will bankruptcy ruin my credit?

A. This is discussed in Chapter 15. In many cases, for people who are hopelessly in debt and practically speaking have no credit, bankruptcy may actually improve their ability to borrow money, especially if they have a job. But please, if you are thinking about bankruptcy, don't worry about more credit. Credit was what got you into trouble in the first place.

Q. Can a married woman apply for credit in her own name?

A. Yes. A new California law prohibits discrimination in credit toward women. No longer can a woman be denied credit where a man would receive it. See Chapter 4.

178

Q. If someone doesn't sue me on an overdue debt for two years after my last payment, does this mean that they can no longer sue?

A. Probably not, unless it was a debt based on an oral contract where the statute of limitations is only two years. Most debts are on written contracts in which case four years must pass after your last payment for a lawsuit to be barred. See Chapter 8.

Q. In a divorce decree my ex-spouse was ordered to pay all of the debts, but she (he) never paid. Now the creditors are coming after me. Can they do this?

A. Yes. The divorce court only had the power to say who was going to pay between you and your spouse. They didn't have the power to extinguish the creditor's right to collect against both of you. You are still obligated to pay the creditor for all of the community property debts that were incurred during the marriage. You do have the right to sue your spouse and collect (if she/he has any assets) for anything you pay to creditors that your spouse was ordered to pay under the divorce order.

Q. I co-signed for my uncle. He can't pay the debt because he got arrested (lost his job, got sick, disappeared, etc.) and now the creditor says I have to pay. I never got any of the goods or money and it would be a great hardship on my family for me to pay. Can they come after me for the money?

A. Yes.

Q. I bought a motorcycle a few years ago and then lost my job. The bank repossessed the bike. They say that they sold it for a lot less than I still owed and now they want the difference which is $500. It doesn't seem fair that I should have to pay $500 now that I no longer have the bike.

A. See Chapter 11. It probably isn't "fair", but nevertheless the bank is acting in a "legal" way. Deficiency judgments of this type have been outlawed for most types of property except motor vehicles, where they are still legal.

F

Fair Debt Collection Practices
  Law 69 fn, 75-77
Federal Equal Credit Opportunity
  Act 45
Federal Trade Commission 19, 77

G

Garnishment 95-105

H

Holder-in-due-course 25
Homesteads 11, 120-121

I

Income taxes 95 fn, 142-144,
  158

J

Judgment creditor 92, 93-94,
  97, 126-127
Judgment proof 15, 164
Judgments 83, 92, 93-94

L

Lawsuits 29, 81-92
Lawyers 26-31, 149, 170
Life insurance 110

M

Marital discrimination 45-47,
  178
Mobile homes 57, 110
Motor homes 57 fn, 61 fn
Motor vehicles 56-63
  attachments 107-108
  deficiency judgment 61-62
  exemption 109
  repair 62-63
  repossession 57-61, 177
  right to reinstate contract 60

Municipal court 82, 83,
  86-92

O

Order of Examination 126-
  128

P

Pensions 110
Personal property 16
Promissory note 16
Property taxes 122

R

Race discrimination 45
Real property 16, 117-125
Recovery fund 125
Redemption 121
Re-financing 123
Repossession 57-61

S

Savings accounts 11, 16,
  110, 112, 156
Second mortgages 123-124
Service of process 82-83, 91
Settlements 72-75
Sex discrimination 45-47
Skip-tracing 69-72
Small Claims Court 21-22,
  77, 82, 83, 86
Social Security 111
Spousal support 95, 150-154,
  158, 178
Statute of Limitations 81,
  141, 177, 179
Student Loans 136-141, 159,
  177, 178
Superior Court 82, 83, 86-
  88

PETER JAN HONIGSBERG is author of **Gilberts, Legal Research,** and **The Unemployment Benefits Handbook,** Addison-Wesley, and co-author of the California Eviction Defense Manual.

RALPH "JAKE" WARNER lives in Berkeley, California. He is concerned with consumer law reform with the goal that everyone will have equal access to our legal system. A people's law pioneer, he helped found Nolo Press and has been active in creating several other alternatives to our constipated and overpriced legal system. Jake is the co-author of **The California Tenants' Handbook, The Living Together Kit, Everybody's Guide to Small Claims Court,** and editor of **The People's Law Review,** a Whole Earth Catalog of the self-help law movement.

NOLO PRESS
SELF-HELP LAW SERIES

Nolo Press publishes a comprehensive series of self-help law books designed to help you untangle the mumbo jumbo and obfuscation that often surround even the simplest of legal procedures. With these books, you are able to take care of many common legal situations, from forming a small corporation to getting a divorce or planning your estate. With attorney's fees running at an inflated $40-$150 an hour, our self-help law series offers a sensible and financially sound alternative. It also provides a means of taking a more active role in the legal matters that affect you.

THE PEOPLE'S LAW REVIEW
An Access Catalog To Law Without Lawyers
Edited by Ralph Warner $8.95

This book is about eliminating the need for lawyers. It gathers resources and ideas that point to ways in which access to everyday law and the resolution of common disputes can be opened to all. Included are materials on doing away with the adversary system, mediation, the possibilities of expanding small claims court, law in China and Cuba as well as nuts and bolts sections that supply practical information on all sorts of legal areas from getting a book copyrighted to handling your legal research.

> "A Whole Earth Catalog of law"
> Time Magazine
> December 8, 1980

Business & Finance

BANKRUPTCY: DO-IT-YOURSELF:

By attorney Janice Kosel. Shows exactly how to file for bankruptcy in California. Comes complete with sample forms and worksheets to compute property and debts, and a complete set of forms which you can tear out and use. Discussion on whether or not bankruptcy makes sense as a solution to your financial problems, when to file, what property you can keep in bankruptcy, and much more. $12.00

BILLPAYERS' RIGHTS

Fourth Edition. A constructive guide for those who find themselves over their heads in legal debts. Contains information on wage and bank account attachments, car repossession, child support debts, student loans, bankruptcy, etc. Also, detailed information on how to deal with collection agencies, including sample letters and agreements. Recommended by the Washington Post, L.A. Times, S.F. Examiner, Berkeley Co-op News and S.F. Action. $6.95

HOW TO FORM YOUR OWN CALIFORNIA CORPORATION:

Third Edition. This extremely popular book, by California attorney Anthony Mancuso, includes tear-out Articles, Bylaws, minutes and stock certificates and all the instructions necessary to set up your own small California corporation. The tax consequences of incorporating are thoroughly discussed. Takes advantage of the 1977 Corporation law. For profit corporations only. $15.00

PROTECT YOUR HOME WITH A DECLARATION OF HOMESTEAD:

Fourth Edition. Your house can be protected from your creditors up to $40,000 under California law only if you file a homestead. Here we tell you how to do it cheaply, easily and legally. An invaluable gift for the new homeowner. Includes recent law changes. Also contains information and forms on exemptions for mobile homes and houseboats. $5.95

SMALL TIME OPERATOR:

How to start your own small business, keep your books, pay your taxes and stay out of trouble. Includes a year's supply of ledgers and worksheets. This book is for people who have an idea, a skill or a trade, and the desire to make their living working for themselves. By Bernard Kamoroff, C.P.A. Distributed by Nolo Press. $7.95

CALIFORNIA NON-PROFIT CORPORATION HANDBOOK:

Second Edition. Completely revised to cover all the new law changes. Step-by-step instructions on how to choose a name, draft Articles and Bylaws, attain favorable tax status, and get your non-profit corporation started. Thorough information on federal tax exemptions which groups outside of California will find particularly useful. $15.00

THE PARTNERSHIP BOOK: HOW TO LEGALLY START YOUR OWN SMALL BUSINESS

By Denis Clifford and Ralph Warner. When two or more people join to start a small business, one of the most basic needs is to establish a solid, legal partnership agreement. This book supplies a number of sample agreements with the information you will need to use them as is or to modify them to fit your needs. Buy-out clauses, unequal sharing of assets, death or withdrawal of a partner, valuation of partnership assets, and limited partnerships are all discussed in detail. Available October, 1981. $15..00

Family & Friends

AFTER THE DIVORCE:

HOW TO CHANGE CUSTODY, SUPPORT AND VISITATION ORDERS: By attorney Joseph L. Matthews. Picks up where How To Do Your Own Divorce leaves off. A concise guide --- with all legal forms and instructions --- explaining how child support can be changed. Also contains new joint custody rules with necessary forms to make custody changes. $12.00

THE PEOPLE'S GUIDE TO CALIFORNIA MARRIAGE & DIVORCE LAW:

By attorneys Ralph Warner and Toni Ihara. Contains invaluable information on community and separate property, names, debts, children, buying a house, etc. Includes sample marriage contracts, a simple will, probate avoidance information and an explanation of gifts and inheritance taxes. $7.95

HOW TO DO YOUR OWN DIVORCE IN CALIFORNIA:

This famous book revolutionized the divorce field by making it clear and simple to the layperson. Tells you the practical things you need to think about and gives information and advice on making your various decisions. Shows exactly how to do your own. Over 200,000 copies in print have saved Californians more than $15 million in attorney fees. New edition includes 1979 law changes. (California only) $8.95

A LEGAL GUIDE TO LESBIAN/GAY RIGHTS:

By attorneys Hayden Curry and Denis Clifford. Discusses in detail such areas as raising children (custody, support, living with a lover), buying property together, wills, etc. Comes complete with sample agreements. This is a national book, produced by Nolo Press and published by Addison-Wesley. $10.95

HOW TO ADOPT YOUR STEPCHILD:

By Frank Zagone. This straightforward guide shows you how to prepare all the legal forms necessary to adopt your stepchild in California. Includes information on how to get the consent of the natural parent and how to conduct an "abandonment" proceeding if necessary. Private and agency adoptions are not covered. $10.00

MEN'S RIGHTS:

By attorney William Wishard. Discusses rights and issues with which men (and women) are concerned: living together, abortion, fatherhood, employment, child custody, support and visitation, and much more. Distributed by Nolo Press. $6.95

Rules & Tools

CALIFORNIA TENANTS' HANDBOOK

Sixth Edition. Sound practical advice on getting deposits back, breaking a lease, getting repairs made, using Small Claims Court, dealing with the obnoxious landlord and forming a tenants' union. Contains numerous sample letters and agreements as well as a Fair-to-Tenants tear-out lease and rental agreement. "...sharper than a serpent's tooth." --- Herb Caen, S.F. Chronicle (over 80,000 in print) $7.95

HOW TO CHANGE YOUR NAME

California Edition. Second Edition. Changing your name is cheap and easy. This book comes complete with all the forms you need to do it yourself. Full information on women's name problems with special attention to women who want to retain, or return to, their own name after marriage or divorce. This book is primarily valuable to Californians. $7.95

DON'T SIT IN THE DRAFT:

By Charles Johnson. A draft counselling guide with information on how the system works, classifications, deferment, exemptions, medical standards, appeals, and alternatives. $6.95

IMMIGRATING TO THE U.S.A.:

This is the best, moderately-priced guide for non-lawyers who are interested in immigration. Written by an experienced immigration lawyer who himself immigrated to the U.S., it discusses student visas, preference categories, marrying a U.S. citizen, work permits, non-immigrant visas, deportation and much more. Immigration forms are reproduced along with instructions on how to fill them out. $9.95

LANDLORDING:

A practical guide for the conscientious landlord and landlady. Covers repairs, maintenance, getting good tenants, how to avoid evictions, record keeping and taxes. "A step-by-step guide to acquisition of business sense." -- San Diego Tribune. This is a large book, 8½ x 11, 253 pages, produced by Express Press and distributed by Nolo. $15.00

RIGHTS OF THE ELDERLY & RETIRED:

Attorney William Wishard has written the first excellent treatment of legal and practical problems that affect the elderly. Included is information on social security, medicine, nursing homes, housing problems and solutions, debt problems, taxes and much more. Anyone who is retired or cares for or loves an older person, will benefit from reading this book. Distributed by Nolo Press. $6.95

MUSICIAN'S GUIDE TO COPYRIGHT:

By Erickson. In just 85 pages, this book does exactly what its title says. It is highly informative and answers most of the important questions a musician will have regarding her/his work. Distributed by Nolo Press. $5.95

EVERYBODY'S GUIDE TO SMALL CLAIMS COURT

Third Edition. Attorney Ralph Warner takes you step-by-step through the Small Claims procedure, providing practical information on how to evaluate your case, file and serve papers, prepare and present a case, and, most important, how to collect when you win. New 50 state Appendix contains information on Small Claims procedures in all states. Separate chapters on common situations such as automobile sales and repair, landlord-tenant, debt cases. $7.95

THE UNEMPLOYMENT BENEFITS HANDBOOK

By attorney Peter Jan Honigsberg. This comprehensive book is a must for anyone who is out of work. It takes you step-by-step through the maze of unemployment laws, and tells you how to find out if you are eligible for benefits & how the amount of benefits is determined. Solid information on filing and handling appeals if benefits are denied, as well as practical advice on how to deal with the bureaucracy. Nationally applicable. $6.95

MARIJUANA: YOUR LEGAL RIGHTS

By attorney Richard Moller. Here is the vital legal information all marijuana users and growers need to guarantee their constitutional rights and protect their privacy and property. It gives the straight facts on the marijuana laws -- what they are, how they differ from state to state, and how legal loopholes can be used against smokers and growers. Good in all 50 states. $6.95

THE TRAFFIC BOOK: HOW TO FIGHT YOUR TICKET AND WIN

By David W. Brown. A comprehensive manual on how to fight your California traffic ticket. Radar, drunk driving, preparing for court, arguing your case to a judge, cross-examining witnesses are all covered in detail. If you have any thought of going into traffic court you will want to have this book under your arm. Available in October, 1981. $8.95

LEGAL RESEARCH: HOW TO FIND AND UNDERSTAND THE LAW

By attorney Steve Elias. A hands-on guide to unraveling the mysteries of the law library. Written for the non-lawyer, this book contains comprehensive practical information on how to research statutes and cases using code books, legal encyclopedias, and other legal reference tools. Available September 1981. $10.00

Wills & Estate Planning

PLAN YOUR ESTATE: WILLS, PROBATE AVOIDANCE, TRUSTS & TAXES

By attorney Denis Clifford. This comprehensive book contains a great deal of legal information about the practical aspects of death. Here in one place for the first time, Californians can get information on making their own will, alternatives to probate, planning to limit inheritance and estate taxes, living trusts, and providing for children. A person's right to die and legal rights to a funeral of his or her own choice are also discussed in detail. This book will greatly increase the information the average person has about estate planning. $15.00

TO ORDER BOOKS:

1 - 9 books: Title(s) of book(s), price,
85¢ postage for first book,
and 35¢ for each additional
book. California residents
include tax (6½% BART & Santa
Clara counties, 6% elsewhere).

10 or more books: Titles of books, price less
20% discount, tax (see above)
(we pay postage)

Send check or money order to either:

NOLO PRESS-COURTYARD BOOKS
950 Parker Street
Berkeley, Calif. 94710
(415) 549-1976

or

NOLO PRESS DISTRIBUTING
Box 544
Occidental, CA. 95465
(707) 874-3105

ORDER FORM

QUANTITY	TITLE	PRICE	TOTAL
	How To Adopt Your Stepchild	10.00	
	After The Divorce	12.00	
	Bankruptcy: Do-It-Yourself	12.00	
	Billpayers' Rights	7.95	
	How To Form Your Own California Corporation	15.00	
	How To Do Your Own Divorce in California	8.95	
	Plan Your Estate: Wills, Probate Avoidance, Trusts & Taxes	15.00	
	*A Legal Guide for Lesbian/Gay Couples	10.95	
	Protect Your Home With A Declaration of Homestead	5.95	
	*Immigrating to the U.S.A.	9.95	
	*Landlording	15.00	
	*The Living Together Kit	8.95	
	*Marijuana: Your Legal Rights	6.95	
	California Marriage & Divorce Law	7.95	
	How To Change Your Name	7.95	
	The California Non-Profit Corporation Handbook	15.00	
	The Partnership Book (available October 1981)	15.00	
	*The People's Law Review	8.95	
	*Rights of the Elderly & Retired	6.95	
	Everybody's Guide to Small Claims Court	7.95	
	*Small Time Operator--Managing Small Businesses	7.95	
	California Tenants' Handbook	7.95	
	The Traffic Book (available October 1981)	8.95	
	*The Unemployment Benefits Handbook	6.95	
	*Men's Rights	6.95	
	*Musician's Guide to Copyright	5.95	
	*Don't Sit in the Draft	6.95	
	*Legal Research	10.00	

* Applicable in all 50 states

Subtotal _____
Tax (see below) _____
Postage (see below) _____

Name_____

Address_____

City_____

State, Zip_____

TOTAL _____

For postage & handling, please enclose 85¢ for the first book and 35¢ for each additional book. California residents include tax (6½% BART & Santa Clara counties, 6% elsewhere).

ABOUT NOLO PRESS

Nolo Press consists of a group of people (some lawyers, some not) who came to see much of what passes for the practice of law as being mumbo jumbo and paper shuffling designed by lawyers to mystify and confuse. Just as the majestic black-robed judge is in reality only a lawyer wrapped in a black shroud, sitting on a wooden platform at the end of a drafty room, a lawyer is all too often a fellow who turns up mumbling esoteric nonsense when ordinary folks take their wallets out.

Started in 1971 with **How To Do Your Own Divorce,** Nolo Press has become a positive energy force for people who want to open up our legal system and make its so-called trade secrets available to all. Nolo has now published close to a dozen books aimed at providing people with the information necessary to help themselves. In the process, it has helped the authors do maintain their own self respect in a field where bank balances have often been more prominent than ethics.

Our books have been written, illustrated, designed and printed by a group of friends headquartered in Berkeley and Occidental, California. Without ever planning to, we have created our own cottage industry. We hope you get as much out of reading this book as we did in making it, and we would be delighted to get any feedback you would care to send our way.